LINCOLN CHRISTIAN COLLEGE

P9-CEB-736

COMMUNICATE
WITH POWER

COMMUNICATE WITH POWER

Insights from America's Top Communicators

EDITED BY MICHAEL DUDUIT

Baker Books

A Division of Baker Book House Co
Grand Rapids, Michigan 49516

©1996 by Michael Duduit

Published by Baker Books
a division of Baker Book House Company
P.O. Box 6287, Grand Rapids, MI 49516-6287

Printed in the United States of America

All rights reserved. No part of this publication may be reproduced, stored in a retrieval system, or transmitted in any form or by any means—for example, electronic, photocopy, recording—without the prior written permission of the publisher. The only exception is brief quotations in printed reviews.

Library of Congress Cataloging-in-Publication Data

Communicate with power : insights from America's top communicators / Michael Duduit, editor.
    p. cm.
   ISBN 0-8010-9017-2 (cloth)
    1. Preaching. 2. Communication—Religious aspects—Christianity.
3. Clergy—United States—Interviews. I. Duduit, Michael, 1954– .
BV4222.C64 1996
251—dc20   96-7608

For information about academic books, resources for Christian leaders, and all new releases available from Baker Book House, visit our web site:
http://www.bakerbooks.com

CONTENTS

94299

PREFACE

The past decade has witnessed a renaissance of interest in biblical preaching in the United States. Across the church—among both evangelicals and mainline denominations—those who had written the obituary of preaching have found their predictions discredited as pastors and laity have rediscovered the power of the proclaimed Word.

Preaching magazine has been a chronicler, encourager, and facilitator of this preaching renewal. Established in 1985, *Preaching* has grown into one of the most widely read journals for today's ministers, and that success has come in large part through a single-minded focus on helping preachers in their task of proclamation.

One of the most popular features in *Preaching* over the years has been our interviews with well-known pastors and Christian communicators. Through the pages of *Preaching,* ministers have had the opportunity to visit with and learn from many of the most gifted preachers in the contemporary church—from John Stott to William Willimon, from Gardner C. Taylor to Chuck Swindoll. Through these interviews, readers have had the opportunity to learn from these models of effective proclamation: how they prepare, how their methods have changed, how they communicate the gospel in today's culture, and much more.

This book is a collection of interviews published during the first decade of *Preaching.* In the earliest years of the publication, most of the interviews were conducted by Dr. R. Albert Mohler, who served as associate editor of *Preaching* for a number of years. Today, he is president of the Southern Baptist Theological Seminary in Louisville, Kentucky. Though no longer a frequent contributor, he continues to be a friend of *Preaching* and writes the annual survey of top books for preachers in our January/February issue.

For the last several years I have had the privilege of conducting most of the interviews. Having the opportunity to visit with some of God's most gifted servants to hear their vision for proclaiming the gospel, to sense their enthusiasm for communicating God's Word has been a remarkable experience. As you read these interviews, I hope you'll also sense the enormous power that comes from the preaching of the Word of God.

Thanks are due to Paul Engle and to Baker Book House for their interest in this project. Throughout the years, their books have provided help and encouragement to many thousands of preachers and church leaders.

Special thanks to the gifted Christian ministers whose insights are found in these pages. They are different in many ways—denominations, church size and worship style, geography and race—but they share one thing: Each has been gifted by God as a communicator of the Word.

Readers interested in learning more about the journal *Preaching* can write to Preaching, P.O. Box 369, Jackson, TN 38302-0369, or call (800) 288-9673. On the Internet you can find *Preaching* at http://www.preaching.com

PREACHING TO CHURCHES
DYING FOR CHANGE

Leith Anderson

Suburban Minneapolis is not known as a hotbed of radicalism—religious or otherwise. But Leith Anderson, whose very name evokes a memory of the area's northern European heritage, says that the church is literally *Dying for Change*. That is, in fact, the title of his book and a prominent theme of his ministry. Anderson is senior pastor of Wooddale Church. Under Anderson's leadership, the church has grown to fourteen hundred members and over three thousand in weekly attendance.

A popular preacher, seminar leader, and educator, Anderson understands the challenge of reaching baby boomers and other largely unchurched groups in modern America. His thoughts on preaching are provocative and penetrating.

Interviewer: Your ministry demonstrates that you take preaching seriously. How do you define the preaching task?

Anderson: I like Phillips Brooks's definition of preaching as "truth mediated through personality." All truth is God's truth—especially as revealed by the Word of God, but the preacher has

9

an essential part in mediating that truth in the context of the preaching event.

Interviewer: You have served Wooddale Church for over a decade, preaching to the same, but ever-growing, congregation. How has your understanding of the preaching task changed over the years?

Anderson: I really don't think that it has changed very significantly. The primary model of preaching I envision does reflect the fact that the world is more complex—so that model is more complex. For example, if you watch reruns of the television show *M*A*S*H,* you know that the plot runs with parallel story lines. Those parallel stories run throughout the program. One story line may be a conflict between two characters, another will look at a moral crisis faced by one of the surgeons, and still another will revolve around a practical joke involving some of the same characters, perhaps with others. But the stories run independently of one another. Some persons watching the show will be drawn to certain story lines, and others will focus elsewhere, according to their interests. I think you will see sermons following the same kind of parallel development.

When I look out over my congregation each service, I see some people with Ph.D. degrees and others who are struggling through life on welfare. There are young people present, along with the old. They have different levels of understanding and education, and they have different needs and concerns. I *must* be faithful to the biblical text—that is primary—but I must also communicate.

I must include stories, humor, and application. The crafting of a sermon is like the weaving of these threads—just like the screenwriter works these parallel story lines into the script.

Interviewer: With that kind of intentionality behind the sermon, how do you prepare your sermons?

Anderson: The topic is usually determined already by the text. I usually preach through books of the Bible, so the text is already in place. When preaching through a book, I start well in advance to collect books and materials on the biblical book. I buy every commentary I can find. When I start on a new series, I may have anywhere from a dozen to twenty commentaries on my desk. By the fourth or fifth sermon, I have usually reduced that stack down to a half-dozen or less that I have found to be of genuine value.

Early on, certain decisions have to be made—ranging from exegetical matters, theme, approach, and so on. Once those decisions are made, they are carried throughout the series, so preaching through a book is going to get easier as the series goes along.

I am convinced, by the way, that this generation is not reached

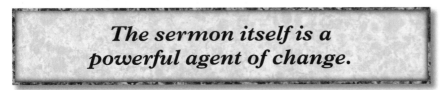

The sermon itself is a powerful agent of change.

by the older style of historical illustrations. References to the Battle of Waterloo or Alexander the Great are really not appreciated or understood. The preacher must find and use illustrations which relate to life as it is experienced by members of the congregation.

Interviewer: Your book, *Dying for Change,* has caught the attention of many preachers, but you do not deal with the preaching event in any detailed focus within that book. To what extent are those issues of change and adaptation relevant to the pulpit?

Anderson: The sermon itself is a powerful agent of change. If the sermon is truth mediated through personality, the truth is understood to be unchanging, but it should focus on the change which must take place in my life and in the life of the community. The truth does not change, but the audience does, and so my presentation of the sermon must also change.

People are looking for a communicator who is much more conversational than the traditional styles allowed. The preacher must be more relational if communication is really to take place. It must be intellectually credible as well as emotionally vibrant. In many churches, the intellectual credibility had been at stake, and the problem was addressed. I think the relational aspect is now the most pressing issue in the communication of the sermon. The times have changed.

Interviewer: How do you trace those changes?

Anderson: I think we can see a recent period in which American churches shifted from a largely nonintellectual approach to a very structured, rationalistic, exegetical, and intellectual program. In more recent years, we are shifting from that approach to a more "seeker-sensitive" model which puts the pressure on being relevant to those outside the traditional church context.

Put bluntly, the shift in recent years has been from Dallas Seminary to Bill Hybels as models. My hope is that we can create an amalgam which can unite the strengths of those approaches. Non-Christians should come to church to find out what the Bible has to say about their deepest problems—the same way they go to a physician to determine their medical problems. We should offer no apologies for communicating biblical truth—but we should do so in a way which is truly relevant, and that is what I am struggling toward. We need a new synthesis.

Interviewer: In the larger context of ministry, how do you envision your pastoral role?

Anderson: The church—our church—needs to be an effective instrument for reaching our community and individual lives for Jesus Christ. We need to recognize that some people who are reached by this church never hear me preach. It's intimidating to come to a worship service, especially at a large church. I really don't think that great churches are built on great preaching alone. I think that day is past. I don't think you can build a great church *without* great preaching, but you can't build a great church without credible ministries beyond the pulpit either.

We must see the congregation in light of the fact that these people have been beat up for six days, and then they come to church with the hope that here they can find a bit of genuinely good news. They *really* want to know that the gospel is good news. That understanding must permeate the life of the church—and not just the sermon.

March/April 1992

BOOMERS, BUSTERS, AND PREACHING

George Barna

George Barna has devoted his career to researching the attitudes of Americans about religious faith and activities. Through a series of best-selling books, such as *The Frog in the Kettle* and *What Americans Believe*, he has communicated the results of his extensive research to church leaders who are struggling with social and demographic change and how those changes affect the church.

Interviewer: You do a great deal of research involving surveys of both churched and unchurched people. Can you offer a brief profile of the churched community in the '90s, in terms of values and practice, based on your research?

Barna: What you find is that they tend to be older than the national norm. They tend to be slightly less well educated, slightly lower in terms of income levels. Women radically outnumber men in terms of the portion of people who are coming. Where values are concerned, it is a group of people who, for the most

13

part, are trying to figure out the purpose of life, and the reason that they are coming to church is to try to get a grip on meaning, a grip on values that will help them make it through the tough stuff they encounter day to day.

We find this especially with people returning to the church who have been away for a while. They are individuals who are coming because they have families, and they perceive that they need help raising those families and inculcating values and a moral perspective on the world.

And in many cases, too, what we find is that there are people who are coming to the church because they want to be part of

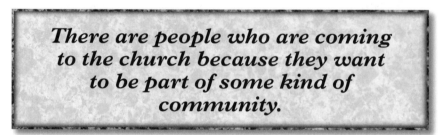

There are people who are coming to the church because they want to be part of some kind of community.

some kind of community. Interestingly, they are not necessarily looking for a community of faith, but they want to become part of a group of people who understand each other and know each other. Then they can start to build meaningful friendships through that network of relationships. So they are looking, in some ways, for different things than the church is trying to foster. Nevertheless, there are certainly opportunities to connect with the sense of needs the people have.

What we are also finding is that when you look at the Christian church in America today, it is not as monolithic or as coherent as it used to be. Today, you have essentially a society which is a disconnected society, and increasingly the churches that people choose to go to are "niche churches." These churches reflect the sociological divisions that are taking place within the culture itself. It is very difficult to come up with a single profile for the church. Look at the churches that we have across the country—there is a much greater variety in terms of worship styles, preaching, styles of Christian education, styles of events, and types of events. The church is much more disparate than it used to be.

Interviewer: Do you find that kind of profile is fairly common as you go from the mainline denominations to evangelical churches?

Barna: Actually, we found those in mainline churches are older than the evangelicals and independents. And in terms of values, there is a very different kind of approach to how they look at the world. Evangelical nondenominational churches tend to be on the conservative side on issues of public policy and personal morality—not as conservative as some people would suggest, but more toward that end.

I think there are definitely some distinctions, even in terms of willingness to embrace change and openness to new forms of technology, with evangelicals more open to change. Mainline churches—from what we have observed at least—seem to be much more reluctant to try a lot of the new stuff, perhaps out of fear that it is going to wind up accommodating a culture as opposed to protecting the truth. A lot of the evangelical churches—certainly not all of them, but a lot—are of the opinion that we can use those new things to help make the truth relevant. These new developments can be used to provide truth without compromising it, by using them simply as tools to that end.

Interviewer: You talk about the development of the "niche churches." Does that signal a limited future for the "old First Church" that has tried to minister to the entire community?

Barna: I think "old First Church" is going to grow differently than it has in the past. What used to take place did so because there was such a homogeneous population. You could let people know the church was in business, and pretty much everybody who lived in the community was similar in some key ways. You no longer have that luxury. Now if you've got one hundred thousand people who live in the community, you probably have one hundred thousand different lifestyles and value systems.

Churches that we're observing are now identifying a niche. The ones that are growing are identifying a niche of people that they want to target and reach; if others come in from outside that niche, that is fine, but the churches are targeting a specific group. Typically what happens is that the church attracts those niche people and then those individuals reach out to their friends (who may be from a related but slightly different niche), thus expanding the boundaries just a little bit. Then those people do the same thing, and the boundaries keep growing. Eventually, what you will wind up with is a large church that is reaching a multitude of niches. It didn't start out that way; it started out being very focused. The church grows because of the network of relationships within it—yet the style and focus of the church's ministry remains pretty much targeted to the initial niche group. The church is still not trying to be all things to all people.

Is the "old First Church" concept dead? No, I don't think so. I think it can still work, but it does need to be fine-tuned; expectations about growth need to be understood within the context of the twenty-first century. It is a very different type of population we are trying to reach. Organizational dynamics are very different. Leadership styles and responsibilities in many ways are very different. I don't think "old First Church" is dead, just different.

Interviewer: How important are doctrinal and theological beliefs to people today?

Barna: Sadly to say, there is very little interest in doctrine or theology. People are interested in practical solutions to their own personal problems. If you can take theology and apply it to those personal concerns and interests, then suddenly people are interested in it. But if you say, "These are the ten basic principles of your faith that you need to know," the first question they will ask is, "Why?" The underlying question to what they ask is, "So what?" They want to know, "What does it have to do with me not getting along with my wife, with my kids being brats, with my job being on the line, with my in-laws saying they want to live with me? Help us with those things," they say, "and then maybe we will have time to listen to your doctrine."

The dangerous implication of this is to see the depth of people's spirituality; it is getting more and more shallow. Then again, that comes back to preaching, teaching, Christian education, and communication. There is a whole different style of communicating in this age, and there is a whole different context that has to be given to people to make theology practical and meaning-ful to them. I think if we could show them "practical" theology, so to speak, there would be a big market for it.

Interviewer: What do you think contributes to that kind of attitude?

Barna: I think a lot of it has to do with the public's overall impression of what takes place in a church when they go there. They come in and they hear music that they don't hear anyplace

> *People are interested in practical solutions to their own personal problems.*

else. They see clothing that they don't see anyplace else. They hear ancient forms of the English language that they don't hear anywhere else. They see all kinds of rituals and traditions—which may be very rich to those who understand them, but most people don't understand them—and there is usually no attempt to help people understand them. So they come in and the first impres-sion they have is, "You know, this is some kind of insider's club that I don't get. I mean, I guess I am welcome here, but why would I come? It doesn't make sense to me."

The second thing that happens is that when we communicate with people, we are again using outdated models. Someone stands up in front of a group of people and talks at them for thirty to forty-five minutes every Sunday, using texts and approaches different from the ones the people are used to hearing. These talks have no apparent relationship, connections, or ties to how they communicate with each other the other six days of the week. Again, what they wind up thinking is, "This doesn't have any-thing to do with me; it's that religious game."

So, I think a lot of that attitude comes from their impression that, "This is church. This is how they do stuff here and it's prob-ably not going to change." Then there are two options—put up with it or get out. I think that is why many people are getting out.

Interviewer: What about the rest of American society in terms of openness to faith? What does your research reflect?

Barna: There is a growing openness to faith—not to Christianity, but to faith—more than at any time over the past quarter century. People are looking for something beyond themselves. I think the '80s was a pivotal decade for America because we kept turning inward. We said we had the solutions to our problems. We thought materialism would do it, individualism would do it; in all kinds of ways we thought we had the answers. Turning inward didn't work and so now people are asking, "Where do I turn?"

People are reluctant to turn to careers or professionalism as being the answer. They know materialism isn't the answer, although they haven't given up on it. Increasingly what we are finding is that people are saying, "There must be something to this spiritual realm. It worked in the past; we don't know how. It is a very different culture today, so spiritualism has to work differently than it used to. Let's try to figure out if there is some way of getting spirituality ingrained in what we are trying to do, to accomplish, and to be."

The baby buster generation, those born since 1965, is a very spiritually intense generation. A major difference is that it is the first American generation—at least that I can tell—that has ever had a starting point for their spiritual journey that was not Christianity. In the past, you started with Christianity and you probably ended up there. Even if you started there and it didn't work for you, at least you had some Christian experience. Now we increasingly see people under the age of thirty who started in other places—maybe with Eastern mysticism, maybe with the Muslim faith, maybe with Buddhism, or another faith system. If those systems don't work, then they may get around to Christianity. But it is no longer a given that one starts with Christianity and branches out.

Interviewer: Any other characteristics of the busters, or Generation X, as it has been called?

Barna: The typical approaches to getting them involved in ministry, in faith, and in spiritual development don't work. For instance, in the past you had what I term "hit-and-run evangelism": You threw the gospel out there and told people to do it or else. Some did it; some didn't. Then you went on to the next group of people. With this generation, that doesn't work at all—their composure is very different, their worldview is very different, and their relational capacity is very different.

What tends to work best with them—from what we can tell so far—is what I call "Socratic evangelism": You keep asking questions and making them think through what it is that they say is their perspective. Eventually, they realize the foolishness of the way they have been thinking about things. Then they come to a responsible conclusion that they possess because they came to it themselves; you didn't give it to them and declare: "Here, take this or else."

The busters are a very discussion-oriented generation, and if you go in and preach at them and say, "This is absolute truth, this is the way to heaven, this is the reality of Jesus Christ, this is the nature of human beings, this is the only way it is," you'll lose them. What you want to do is bring up the question and say, "Let's talk for a while about the nature of truth. What do you believe about truth?" Let them put their values on the table and in a nonthreatening manner say, "Now that is very interesting. I don't happen to believe that might be true, but help me understand your point of view. Tell me about that." Then go back and probe a little bit more on the different descriptions and definitions that they give to you and say, "If that is true, then how does that fit with this other thing that you told me? I am not saying it doesn't; I just need you to help me understand how that works." Keep the conversation going back and forth.

If that approach is going to work with Generation X, the question is, Will the church do it? Right now in America, the Christian church is not poised to engage in that kind of dialogue for several reasons. First, the church typically doesn't make relationships its first priority; it does its speaking act first and, if you accept that, it makes relationships. Second, the approach suggests that we have to have Christians who are willing to engage in dialogue about their faith, which for the most part, we don't. Most people like to learn about faith and then they kind of tuck it away in their hearts. That is not sufficient. Christians have to do something with their faith other than just have it infiltrate their daily actions.

The third difficulty has to do with being able to articulate our faith. One of the most interesting things we do in our research is to ask people to articulate what they believe and why. It is interesting, but it is extraordinarily depressing because what I find is

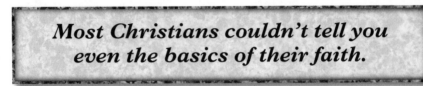

Most Christians couldn't tell you even the basics of their faith.

that most Christians couldn't tell you even the basics of their faith. Most people don't know what is in the Bible; they don't know why they supposedly believe what is in the Bible; they aren't able to explain to other people what is in the Bible; and they couldn't explain to a buster—or anybody else who doesn't believe that the Bible is absolute truth—why it is possible that there could be such a thing as absolute truth and that it might be found in Scripture.

I am concerned, gravely concerned, about the future of the church in America because the culture has been changing and, while we cannot accommodate to society's values, we do need to revisit our methods, which we are not poised to do.

Interviewer: Are there any churches out there that are modeling what you describe?

Barna: There are some that are doing it well. But I am of the opinion, having studied a lot of this stuff, that there is no single model that is the right one to follow. For instance, a lot of people would look at Willow Creek Community Church and say, "Boy, what a great model. Why can't all churches be like that?" I used to attend Willow Creek. I love Willow Creek. I think it is one of the great churches on the face of the earth. But I would be horrified if every church in America that was being planted or that underwent some kind of internal renewal tried to become Willow Creek II. Given the kinds of resources, leadership, and community niche of Willow Creek, it would be very inappropriate for another church to emulate it. Willow Creek is one very appropriate model for certain types of ministries, but not for all types.

There are other models out there which probably aren't as well known nationally. But frankly, because every community is becoming so heterogeneous, I think it is imperative that we raise up church leaders who are not looking to mimic what other churches are doing, but are willing to go out and study them and try to figure out the principles that can be taken away to help them contextualize without compromise. They should lead without accommodating everybody, and be an authentic church while having some of the idiosyncrasies that reflect the kind of people that they want to reach. It is going to take a lot of creativity, innovation, and courage to make the church go forward in the twenty-first century.

Interviewer: A lot has been written about the baby boomers, and now we are beginning to see books on the baby busters. Could you compare and contrast the two generations? Is it possible for the same church to do an effective job of reaching both?

Barna: It would be very, very difficult for the same church to reach the boomer and the buster. First of all, there is an animosity between the two generations. Second, their styles of communication are different. Third, the ways in which they define success are different. Fourth, their lifestyles are very different. I have looked at a lot of churches that claim they are reaching both generations and, frankly, when you come right down to it, there are at best a handful of churches around the country that are doing it well.

I think you almost have to develop independent congregations, which may be under the same umbrella. It may all be "First Church," but there is probably a congregation of boomers, a congregation of busters, a congregation of builders, and a congregation of seniors all under that umbrella. The builders and seniors can live with anybody, as long as you don't play rock music. But the builders and busters really clash—their heroes are different, the kind of information processing skills they have are different, the types of preaching they respond to are different, their willingness to read Scripture is different, and even their literacy skills are very different. No, I don't think that the best approach is to try to build a church that is going to bridge the gap between the two; unless, perhaps, you have a cause that is going to be so compelling to both generations in your particular community that they will be willing to put aside all their other differences and get behind a cause—a social cause that is going to attract them.

What we have found, though, is that busters also are different from boomers in that they are very much cause-driven, just like the boomers were at the same life stage. The difference is that busters' intensity in that cause is more short-lived. They will be

> *It is going to take a lot of creativity, innovation, and courage to make the church go forward in the twenty-first century.*

intense on any given issue that they choose to embrace for about nine to twelve months. After that it is out of their lives; they are on to something else. And many of the busters get out of the whole cause-driven lifestyle at that point anyway. So, I am not sure that trying to rally the boomers and the busters around a cause is a good tactic for trying to build a church. It is one way of attracting both at the same time; but I am not sure it is good long-term strategy.

Interviewer: Given all these different things that are going on with the various generational segments, what kind of counsel do you give to preachers who are trying to understand and minister effectively in the '90s? For example, you talked about communication styles; which ones are more effective in the current climate, according to your research?

Barna: In thinking generationally, I would say to somebody who wants to reach the busters: Understand first of all that they think differently than every other generation we know. Also, one of the realities of their lives is that they communicate differently, and for the church to have a lasting impact and a lasting relationship with them, we need to reflect a sensitivity to that. Thirty- to forty-minute sermons don't work with busters. Doing a service which does not incorporate video and contemporary music for the most part does not work with busters. Having a church which is not relational and accomplishment oriented doesn't work with busters. Busters are terribly relational; they're looking for that much more than other people.

Some of the fascinating churches I have visited that are trying to reach busters and are doing so successfully may have a thirty-minute sermon, which is broken into three segments during the course of the service. You have a ten-minute introduction to the topic, then you have an eight-minute video on that topic. Then the preacher comes back and preaches another ten minutes. Then you have a drama sketch for five to eight minutes, and the service is closed with ten minutes of preaching. That fits their communication style and their attention span. It fits their style of thinking—the "mosaic" style of thinking.

For boomers my advice is: Give them the problem; don't give them a solution. Busters are not assured that you are ever going to give them the solution. They are much happier with an open-ended sermon where you have raised the issue, where you have given them stuff to chew on, and then you have given them opportunities through other forms of the ministry to come back and deal with it. But to stand there and say, "Here is the problem; here is the solution," doesn't work very well with them.

Boomers can sit still for a longer period of time. They can do the twenty- to thirty-minute sermon; beyond that they tend to get antsy. There is a whole different approach in terms of what they are looking for; they want references—almost a scholarly approach to what they are being given. But I would say the thing that both of these generations (busters and boomers) have in common has to do with what they see modeled in the life of the person who is teaching. They want somebody who is realistic, who is vulnerable, who is struggling, and who is saying, "I have not mastered it, but this is where I am at this point in time. I think this is a useful strategy or perspective. I don't have it totally together; grow with me."

You have seen what has happened with some of the media preachers. What we are finding is that while people don't necessarily hold the behavioral patterns of Jimmy Swaggart, Jim Bakker, and the rest of them against the church, there is a sense of skepticism about any one person having it all together and one's ability to dispense from on high all the truth that another needs to know about any given topic. Increasingly, we just don't buy that. So in that sense, I think, having the authoritative spellbinder standing up front is anachronistic.

What I have started to do, in my books and teaching, is to try to help people understand the underlying principles so they will go out and explore church models. I love for pastors and other church leaders to get out there and see what else is going on. Yet as I talk with pastors, they are so protective of the pulpit that they are afraid to leave four or five times a year to see—and experience—what other churches are doing. You have to do that.

Try to convince me that GM doesn't buy at least one model of every Ford, Toyota, and Nissan that comes out so they can tear it apart and inquire how they are doing. Of course they do that! Nabisco does the same thing with every product that comes out of General Mills and General Foods. We have to do the same thing; not because we are in competition, but because we want to learn, we want to explore, we want to really experience what else God could be doing through us. It is an educational process.

September/October 1994

PREACHING TO PAGANS

Steve Brown

Steve Brown is one of the most compelling communicators within the evangelical community. He sports a mischievous smile and a resonant bass voice that must have come in handy in his radio disc jockey days. In 1990, Steve resigned the pastorate of Key Biscayne Presbyterian Church in Key Biscayne, Florida, to devote full-time to his growing ministry through radio (as speaker for KeyLife Ministries), conferences, and as a professor of homiletics at Reformed Theological Seminary in Orlando.

Interviewer: In your book entitled *If Jesus Has Come: Thoughts on the Incarnation for Skeptics,* I was intrigued by the idea of preacher as former skeptic. Do you think your experience as an adult unbeliever causes you to preach differently? As I recall, you came to a real faith encounter with Christ after you were in the pastorate. How do you think that makes your preaching different than it might be otherwise?

25

Brown: I think there are a couple of things. I went into the far country—I was in commercial broadcasting. In that trek, I learned to think like a pagan and talk like a pagan and to understand where the buttons of pagans need to be pushed. I learned the places where their hearts are broken and what keeps them awake at night. And so I learned a pagan mind-set in those days. I learned where their doubts were coming from, and often said if I ever got answers to those honest questions, I'd provide some answers for other people who are asking honest questions. I'd go around and say, "How do you believe?" and people would say, "Well, you've just got to believe." That's like saying to a drowning man, "If you would swim then you wouldn't drown," and he knows that.

There are churches that are seeker-driven and those that are seeker-sensitive. My experience makes me not seeker-driven, but certainly seeker-sensitive in terms of what the average person is thinking. The interesting thing is that most Christians don't think much differently than pagans. We have this tendency to say that our flock is so much different than the world, but sometimes it's hard to tell the difference.

Interviewer: What do you think are some of those questions that pagans are dealing with that preaching perhaps avoids or ignores?

Brown: Whatever you think about the recovery movement, somebody has developed a marketing miracle in the sense that they have found out where the needs are. This recovery thing—the Twelve Step program—is absolutely sweeping across the country. I teach a seminar with seven steps—it's sort of an economy size! I also have a 99 percent tithe and that sort of thing.

I think we need to see the recovery movement in terms of some of the basic needs for which the Scriptures provide answers, because it's *the* owner's manual. Sometimes we have developed a mind-set where we really think it's important whether or not the Graf-Wellhausen documentary hypothesis is true, or whether anybody knows about the five points of Calvinism, or whether anybody even cares what strict subscriptionism is or what the regulative principle is. That isn't where people are. We're fighting those battles that were fought long ago—and I doubt whether a whole lot of people cared even then—instead of watching and saying, "There are people who are oppressed, who are dying, who are abused, who feel so guilty they can hardly breathe," and then bringing answers to people like that.

I think we, as Christians, provide legitimate, balanced answers for the questions that are being asked by people in the recovery movement. One of the dangerous things about the recovery movement is people become addicted to that, and it becomes another area of control—even another area of abuse. We, as Christians, can say, "Look, you're asking the right questions because God gave you the questions, but we have some different answers." And I think preachers who are wise will listen to those questions and then see if our material meets those needs—and it does, by the way.

I don't think we need to always change our material. We're not market-driven in the sense that we find out whatever they need and then we provide it. I think that's from the pit of hell and smells like smoke. But I do think that we listen to the pain of the world and then we go to God's Word and we say, "Does it speak to this pain?" and it does—it just does, it really does!

Interviewer: One of the things that I've always been struck with in your preaching is the strength of your illustrations. Other pastors who have listened to you say the same thing. I've wondered how much of your particular use of illustration comes out of that pagan perspective.

Brown: I think a lot of it does. As you know I teach at Reformed Theological Seminary. I teach the T.U.L.I.P. of communication. The "I" of the tulip is illustrate, illustrate, illustrate! I say to the students, "If you can't illustrate it, it's not true." See, we forget that doctrine isn't for doctrine's sake, and that theological propositions aren't for theological propositions' sake. Those are ways whereby we communicate the reality that we've discovered, and that reality's a time-space thing, and if you can't illustrate it, it's not true. If you can't illustrate it, then don't teach it, 'cause it doesn't make any difference.

My mentor early in my ministry—and I don't have a particular gift at that, I think it's a learned kind of thing—John Stanton, who's in heaven now, talked to me a lot. He said, "You have two problems with your preaching. The first is you use words that nobody understands. The second is you don't tell them how to make it work by illustrating it. If you'll fix that, God can use

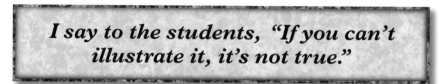

I say to the students, "If you can't illustrate it, it's not true."

you." He taught me how to illustrate. He used to quote Barnhouse, who I quote now, that all of life illustrates Bible doctrine. I carry a notebook with me, and there isn't a conversation I can't get an illustration from—including this one. When we started talking, the tape came unraveled and you had a spare. I can get an illustration out of that; I can teach biblical truth with that—the way you had a spare. There are so many things that we can teach through something like that. What you need to do is say, "God make me sensitive to real life so that I can illustrate your truth."

You buy a lot of illustration books too. I tell you, at seminary your homiletics professor probably said, "It is beneath a man of God to use an illustration book." He's lying, folks. He's lying through his teeth. If you get one good illustration out of an illustration book, it's worth every dime you paid for it. Read, always read. Don't stop reading and you'll get illustrations; God always uses them. If we don't illustrate, we ought not teach.

Interviewer: Describe for me the process that you use in actually preparing your sermons.

Brown: It's not esoteric; it's pretty standard. There is a supernatural step that I kind of sense happens. I teach through the books of the Bible—at least I did when I was a pastor—I'm doing more subject-oriented stuff now, but it's still biblical teaching. It's built around a certain track. Always in the pulpit as a pastor, I would go through books of the Bible. I didn't break that except on Christmas Sunday and Easter Sunday. I didn't do the Lenten series and I didn't do Mother's Day—I would pray for those things. We emphasized the teaching of the Bible: Where we stopped last week, that's where we're going to start this week.

I've always had a very extensive library in the area where I was teaching because I always bought the books to meet that. So I read everything I could get on a particular text, took notes on it, and then I wrote down truths that I'd learned—things that would make a difference in people's lives because they would make a difference in my life. Then I would fill up three or four pages of a legal pad with those kinds of notes. I made it a point to ask, "Is there any question that could be asked about this text by the people I teach that I couldn't answer?" And if there was any question that came to mind that I didn't have an answer for, I kept searching until I had it all. If I had time, I did a word study. I used Kittel's *Theological Dictionary of the New Testament.* I did all the stuff everybody does; then I put it aside. I'd say, "God, the gasoline's in the engine. Now if you want this car to go, you hit the starter and I'll do whatever you want me to do with it."

I don't want to sound super-spiritual, but more often than not it has been like a light, like a knowing, and you say, "Yeah, that's the way I'm going to deal with that." Then I would build an outline from that. Once the outline was settled, then I hung meat on it. That's pretty pedestrian; that's pretty much the way most preachers deal with it.

Interviewer: How far in advance was this process going on before you actually stood in the pulpit?

Brown: At least an hour! I am not a good model. I get intimidated by guys who say, "I golf in the summer and plan my preaching for the next year." Good Lord, I don't know what I'm going to say next Sunday and I certainly don't remember what

> *We're in dangerous territory when we look to impossible models as preachers.*

I said last Sunday! Generally, I made sure that I had a day for each presentation, and that day might end up being five hours. Then God gave me an extra two or three hours that I could have fun in, go to a movie or be with my family. But sometimes that day would start at four in the morning and it would be three in the morning before I finished. But I left that day open without any interruptions.

Usually I preached on Wednesday night and Sunday morning and I left a full day to prepare for those. The good thing for me in terms of going through books of the Bible was that I always knew what the next one was going to be, because I just did the next paragraph—that process is not to be emulated; it's wrong. I always teach the students how to do it and say, "Look, don't follow me because I'm lost sometimes!"

Interviewer: Henry Ward Beecher would work all through the week. He would get up Sunday morning and after breakfast he'd prepare his sermon for that Sunday morning. He would have been collecting material and he'd get up Sunday morning and that's when his preparation process began. But he would say at that point, Sunday morning, it was a matter of deciding what he *wasn't* going to talk about because he'd already been mulling it over and dealing with it during the week.

Brown: And he had a tremendous mind. I think that's one of the things we have to be careful about. I'm an ordinary guy who works hard. I work really hard. People think that because my preaching is rather laid-back, my preparation is laid-back. It's not. It's a studied laid-backness and I work my tail off to make that happen. You get a guy like Beecher who says that's how he preaches, but you have to remember that they don't come along but once in a generation. We're in dangerous territory when we look to impossible models as preachers. Guys, you gotta work. You gotta put your fanny in the chair and work your tail off. Then you gotta put your knees on the floor and cry up to God for help. Sometimes it happens and sometimes it doesn't.

Interviewer: Even though you're not pastor of a local church—you're teaching preaching, you're ministering through KeyLife—you're still preaching a lot. How do you find that your preaching is changing as compared to when you were doing it for the same congregation?

Brown: It's more focused and I don't have a lot of assumptions about the people to whom I talk. You know, when you've been a pastor of a church for eighteen years, they really groove with you. You could almost give the number of the joke and they'd laugh, because we'd been together so long. I know where the hot spots are and they know the basics—they know that I'm a Calvinist, that I'm quite Reformed in my teaching. I don't have to say, "This is the reason I'm saying this."

By and large, now I spend my time on the road teaching and preaching and speaking. I recognize that I can't make those assumptions of other people, so I start more from scratch. I'm far more focused subject-wise than I would be in a local church, because I know I'm gonna get one shot. So if I'm going to say something important, I've gotta say it now because I won't be able to do it next Sunday.

Interviewer: Has the nature of your sermons themselves changed a good bit? You had a traditional pattern—you'd have some preliminary thoughts that didn't actually fit into the outline, but some of the best stuff was in that section; then you'd have your biblical outline. Have you changed that style?

Brown: Not a whole lot. I still will take a text that deals with the subject and still feel guilty because there's stuff sticking out of the suitcase that I feel like I ought to say something about. So that form is pretty much the form in which I still teach. I'm doing two-day seminars all over the country. Now, they aren't like that. They involve teaching very defined, cognitive material over a two-day period.

Interviewer: If you were going to pass along some suggestions to young preachers about their preaching ministry, what thoughts would you offer them?

Brown: What happens when you start teaching homiletics is that your mind gets so filled with so much stuff that needs to be said that it's hard to focus on something. I would say: Be the personification of what you preach. When I say that, I don't mean in the old sense of modeling holiness. I'm talking about the kind of vulnerability and honesty that you appreciate in others—be that in the pulpit. There's a danger when preaching because the pulpit grants us a place to pontificate, to play games, and to look down arrogant noses at the poor peasants in the pew.

In the church that I served, I came up from the congregation to preach. I had a petition put on my desk by a number of people in the church who wanted me to sit up front behind the pulpit the way one always did before a sermon. I tore it up, because I realized the reason they wanted me to sit there says something really bad about them and about preachers. So I would sit in the congregation, and when it was my time to teach the Bible, I walked up to the pulpit—well, we didn't have a pulpit. I usually sat on a bar stool and taught. It was a statement: "Guys, as I teach you this stuff, you need to know that I'm placing myself under the authority of God's Word, too. I've worked through some of this; I'll be honest when I'm not living it. I'll tell you where I am living it. I'll tell you what's helped me and made the difference. But above all, this is revealed propositional truth and we don't have the freedom to change it."

That's the kind of modeling that I think is good for a pastor. I think there were days in the past when pastors and preachers could pontificate—Beecher was one of those, Harold John Ockenga was one of those, Harry Emerson Fosdick was one. I think our day and age has forced us to take the armor off; the preacher who doesn't will die.

November/December 1992

Do a Little Every Day

Fred B. Craddock

Few readers will be unfamiliar with the contributions of Fred Craddock to the world of preaching and homiletics. His stature among preachers continued to increase with the impact of his work, *Preaching,* the 1986 Book of the Year for *Preaching* magazine.

Now retired from his post as professor of preaching and New Testament at the Candler School of Theology at Emory University, Craddock has a national and international influence through his books and video series.

Interviewer: Those who have observed the emergence of your preaching model can detect a rather pronounced shift in your estimation of the stature of preaching within the Christian community.

In your book *As One without Authority,* you began with a chapter entitled "The Pulpit in the Shadows." Your later work suggests a much more optimistic evaluation. How do you see the current state of preaching?

Craddock: Well, I certainly would not choose a chapter heading like that today. The departments of preaching in the seminaries are well staffed. Schools that did not require a single course in preaching for the last twenty years now require three, six, or even nine hours in preaching.

Beyond that, the electives in preaching are well populated in schools across the country, and many schools are trying to find more teachers of preaching; so the days of the doldrums and caricatures, jokes, put-downs, and condescension have subsided. The situation is much different now, many years since I wrote *As One without Authority.*

Interviewer: That addresses the academic stature of preaching among the other theological disciplines. What about the current state of preaching as a church office?

Craddock: Preaching is much stronger. The increased expectation of the congregation is finding its response. I find a great deal of strong preaching among younger ministers. There are ministers in their forties and fifties who never had any training in preaching through their seminary experience in the 1960s. They just did not put much stock in it and went instead into counseling or a one-on-one ministry. The "sit-down ministry" among some of those in their late forties and early fifties is very

> *Preaching generates a high level of expectation like no other single act in the church.*

good. But this younger crowd, the twenty-five- to forty-year-olds, includes many really strong preachers who strive to improve their preaching. The church appreciates this. This group would include a good many Catholic priests too.

This is not to say that there are no good or great preachers among the older generation; that is not true. But the appreciation for preaching has demonstrably increased and ministers are responding to that challenge.

Interviewer: William Muehl's last book was entitled *Why Preach? Why Listen?* That puts the issues right before us. Why do we preach?

Craddock: Well, because we must. We must join the biblical Word with the human voice of the believer standing up in the company of other believers. Preaching has a socializing, community-building force. It brings the page of the text to life in an oral way. The nuances of the human voice maximize the content of the biblical message.

Preaching has a heavy tradition that generates a high level of expectation like no other single act in the church. Wherever you have an expectation this high, the possibility of gain, of fruit, of change, is great.

Interviewer: Your model of preaching defies many traditional categories used to describe dimensions of the preaching task, including categories of sermon styles—thematic, topical, expository, and other labels. What categories do you find useful?

Craddock: That is a good question. I really do not often think in those terms. I think more in terms of a response to the questions: What is the minister seeking to say? and What is the minister seeking to do? By "do," I mean encourage, enlighten, correct, celebrate, confront. I think in terms of these functional categories.

Interviewer: One of the most interesting sections of your most recent book is on the centrality of the life of study in the context of the life of the pastor. You have a most interesting section on time in study as time with the congregation. A good many preachers feel sequestered in their studies—and in competition with other pastoral duties. Is time spent in sermon preparation *really* time spent with the congregation?

Craddock: Through preaching, you share the time spent in the study with the whole congregation. This time should be placed over against time spent studying something which will be shared in a one-on-one session. Therefore, there is more justification for studying two hours every morning, if it is to be shared in preaching and teaching, than for taking time to read this good book for a session with one person. I don't want to minimize that, but studying is time I am going to spend in preparation for the general gathering of the church—where the fruits of that study will be shared. It is not time spent apart from the congregation. The congregation is, in a sense, present with you as you study in this manner.

Interviewer: Most preachers feel a sense of guilt that they do not spend enough time in study. This is a difficult question, but how much study do you see as an adequate level of preparation for the challenge of the preaching task?

Craddock: It seems to me that if the minister gives two hours for study every morning, he can do it, she can do it. This leaves evening and other leisure hours for other kinds of reading. In this morning period, I mean just the hard study—not a lot of fun, but the necessary heart of it. If you go from seven-thirty to nine-thirty or eight to ten every morning, the accumulated benefit of that will be enormous. You can pick up just where you left off. If it is a regular thing, it can become more study than some individuals did during their entire school experience. The regularity is very important and gives you the maximum benefit of accumulated insight. I think if the preacher will do this, the preacher will know a great deal, share a great deal, and be well prepared.

Interviewer: You are a gifted preacher as well as a teacher of preachers. The fruit of your preaching demonstrates a great ability to draw material from your reading in the past—your cogitations, your seasoned thoughts. Do you have any particular secret for your ability to access that material?

Craddock: No, I don't. It is embarrassing that I don't. I keep two kinds of raw material in front of me. I have a notebook in which I scribble things I come across—journalistic pieces, news items, commentary materials, or just informational items. I write them in that notebook or in something else where I can find them.

Then, in addition, I have a journal that is the germinal reflection on what I have read, with whom I have talked, and what I have done. It is almost like a diary, but this journal is the medium for many items, otherwise merely informational, which eventually will find themselves in a sermon.

Interviewer: You are a biblical scholar by training and have an obvious love for genuinely biblical preaching. How would you define biblical preaching over against other possible forms of preaching?

Craddock: I think biblical preaching is that form of preaching which gets both the content and the purpose of the message from the text itself. This comes through a process of understanding the text. What is the text trying to do? Is that what I am trying to do? What does the text say? Is that what I am saying? Those questions expose the meaning and purpose of the text and lead to biblical preaching, whatever the form of the sermon.

Interviewer: In your discussion of qualities to be sought in a sermon, you include several one would expect to find and others which were a surprise. I was particularly struck by two qualities you identified: recognition and anticipation. I would guess that many preachers might not think of these two qualities in the preparation of a sermon. Would you elaborate on these qualities and their importance in preaching?

Craddock: I think the importance of recognition is apparent whenever the congregation is in view. Here, out in front of the preacher, is a body of Christian people, many of whom have been Christians for a long time. What does it say to them if I get up there and give a message in which they don't recognize the material or the message?

I think most of what I say, maybe 90 percent, would be recognizable. The person could say, "Why yes, I knew that." The other 10 percent of the message is then an opportunity for growth. But if the preacher presents a message dominated by material the congregation does not recognize, they will not hear the message. If people have been in this church for thirty years and cannot recognize a thing the preacher is saying—if they do not recognize it at all—they will do one of two things: They will get mad at the preacher, or they will feel put down and stupid. Both of these are incredibly unhealthy.

Now, on the other hand, anticipation is that quality which keeps the congregation listening to the sermon. It lets the listeners know that something is happening here—we are going somewhere, there is a destination, this preacher has something in mind they want to hear—and it keeps them listening. It is the same quality that keeps you watching a television program or reading a good novel. There must be something which will be worked out through the sermon.

Interviewer: Would you see anticipation more easily developed in an inductive sermon or in a deductive model?

Craddock: The inductive sermon is constructed to do precisely this, to move from recognition to discovery. Built into this process is a healthy dose of anticipation.

Interviewer: Though many preachers have learned much from the inductive model, and many have shifted to a model

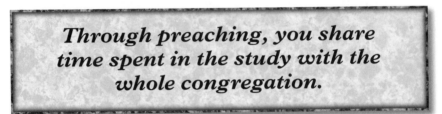

Through preaching, you share time spent in the study with the whole congregation.

which relies primarily on that method, many were trained in the deductive model. Indeed, most preachers find themselves using a deductive model from time to time. Is anticipation impossible in a deductive model?

Craddock: It is not impossible in a deductive model. By the way, you can give the appearance of a deductive sermon and shift with an almost parabolic force. For instance, Robert Funk has a little syllogism: "All sinners are punished. Jim is a sinner. Jim is punished." But suppose you present it: "All sinners are punished. Jim is a sinner. Jim is forgiven." It then has another turn and breaks the syllogism. The anticipation of this turn is true anticipation and can be built into any kind of sermon.

Interviewer: You have located the Word of God at the ear of the listener rather than at the mouth of the preacher. What does this mean for the preacher who wants to be biblical? How does the preacher envision the task of preaching with the realization of the Word at the congregation's ears?

Craddock: What it means is this: If I know the hearers intimately, the good and the bad, I can therefore anticipate any obstacles to good communication. I can anticipate the questions, the objections, and I will voice them for my hearers as I lay out this message.

The preacher needs to know the likely response to the message and build this knowledge into the sermon. If I know when the congregation is likely to think, "Now I hear what you are saying, but it will not really work when you get down to it," I will anticipate this and be ready to voice this objection, along with a response: "But have you thought of this?" I may be able to open their ears, and they might then be able to hear the message. If I don't voice their objection, but leave them sitting there with it, it becomes a barrier. This barrier will prevent the Word of God from lodging in the listeners.

Interviewer: The fact that the reader has found his or her way into this book indicates an interest in preaching. What would be your message to these readers?

Craddock: The primary thing I would say, I suppose, would be a word of encouragement to the preaching minister to find a way in their present setting to have a regular, habitual discipline of study, reading, prayer, and reflection. Do a little bit every day and do not allow yourself to give it second place by that immensely intimidating task of "getting up a sermon." Do a little every day.

March/April 1988

A Vision for Preaching

Frank Harrington

For over two decades, Frank Harrington has stood before the congregation of Atlanta's Peachtree Presbyterian Church. A widely respected and admired churchman, Harrington is a gifted preacher who has led Peachtree to its status as the largest Presbyterian congregation in the nation.

Peachtree Presbyterian Church is located in the midst of Buckhead, an area of Atlanta that blends old Georgia with the New South.

Interviewer: How do you envision the preaching task? How do you see that task week by week as you proclaim the Word at Peachtree?

Harrington: My own view is that preaching is the central task of the preacher. All else in ministry radiates from the effectiveness of the man or the woman in the pulpit. The pulpit is your best opportunity to be an evangelist, your best opportunity to be a pastor, your best opportunity to be a prophet. The pulpit sets the tone for the parish.

The preacher ought to consider himself as God's chief dreamer in his church—as the standard to articulate the dream God has placed on the heart, so that preacher and people together can make the dream come true. That is the central task of the preaching minister.

Interviewer: How does that vision of preaching inform what you do each week?

Harrington: I have been privileged to serve this church now for two-thirds of my professional life. I have been pastor here for many years, and this environment has been encouraging. This church has encouraged me to articulate the dreams and hopes that God has laid upon my heart for these people. People and preaching always go together.

We have all heard the line that the preacher is invisible during the week and incomprehensible on Sunday. That is nonsense. The preacher must prepare, as Karl Barth said, with the Bible in one hand and the newspaper in the other. There is a profound truth there. If you're not in constant touch with people—knowing their hurts, their hopes, their dreams, the rigors of the reality in which they are living—you may find yourself in the pulpit answering questions that no one is asking.

I prepare my preaching a year in advance. I know where I'm headed—I know what specific subject, topic, and text that I'm going to be addressing on a given Sunday a year in advance. I actually write my sermon three months in advance so that I'm never operating under the pressure of next Sunday. That doesn't work for everybody, but I work best when I'm not under the deadline of next Sunday. It also preserves my availability to people. I know that come Sunday morning, a lot of people will be in that sanctuary ready for whatever it is I've got to say. So I arrange my schedule to write ahead of time so that I'm never under the pressure of next Sunday.

Now if something should come up—like the war in the Persian Gulf—of course I interrupt my announced schedule to address that reality. I preached three Sundays in a row on sermons I wrote each week as we were moving toward that war. The Sunday after we were, in fact, involved in combat, I spoke to the situation that was on everybody's mind. You have to do that from time to time. Events intrude upon any schedule. Human need knows no agenda.

I remember one weekend in my second pastorate where two young men were killed under tragic circumstances and a third young man was critically injured and left with permanent disabilities. I knew that the whole focus of the entire family of faith represented in my church would be on those events. So I changed my sermon that night and wrote a sermon on the great text, "Lord to whom shall we go, for thou hast the words of eternal life." Events interrupt our sermons.

In preparation for preaching, I keep in mind that I am away several months in the summer. In the process of planning, I will write seventy-five to one hundred people in this congregation and in the community—including people I may have heard from through our televised services—and ask them a simple question: "If you had the responsibility of standing in the pulpit of Peachtree Presbyterian Church next year, what themes would you emphasize?" I print that question on the front of the church bulletin a couple of times. Interestingly enough, when I first started that, the responses just started trickling in. Now I get an avalanche of mail from a wide variety of people and sources, and I receive some most insightful ideas to develop.

Interviewer: What is the method used for preparing your messages, once you've identified what they're going to be? You often preach in a series pattern.

Harrington: In the course of a year, I'll have two or three series. That would be a major portion of my preaching. I have discovered that worship attendance is better during the series. My series generally are centered on two realities—the part of the church year which is Advent and the part of the church year which is Lent. Then, of course, it is now an annual tradition here that I also preach a series on relationships. I cover a lot of territory in my relationships series. That series just ended with a service in which we renewed our marriage vows. But within that series on relationships I had a sermon on euthanasia, because that's an issue that's in the framework of family relationships these days. I also preached a sermon with the title, "Is Any Sex Safe?" I cover a lot of territory.

In preparing to preach, I read widely and constantly. I read at least three books a week. I'll read biographies, best-sellers, both fiction and nonfiction—I read all of that. I read the books I know other people read. I read widely, and I think reading is mandatory for the minister.

If a congregation were to ask me if there is any one essential thing they ought to do for a minister, I would certainly put high on that list: Be sure that minister has enough financial resources to buy books, and help him to find the time to read them. I carry a stack of books with me everywhere I go. You will see that you can get in a lot of reading time that way. I read early in the morning and I read at night when I'm at home. You might look down at your watch, for example, and say, "It's twenty minutes until lunchtime, no need to get started on anything." What I would do instead is pick up a book and read, because I've always got my books with me.

Interviewer: What kind of materials do you use in the actual preparation of your sermon? Once you've identified the issue— whether it's a series or a stand-alone sermon—once you have identified the focal point, do you begin with a text? Do you begin with a topic? And once you have the two joined together, how do you work through the preparation and construction of the sermon?

Harrington: Well, it could work both ways. I may have a text that has just created an irresistible urge in me or I may have a topic that I'm thinking about, so I will find a text. Either way, I always begin with the text; the first part of my preparation is that I *read* the text. I read it in several translations, and when I'm reading it, I'm just reacting spontaneously to what is there. If something hits my mind about the text, I will jot down my spontaneous reaction. I may check the original languages in this verse, and then put it aside and come back to it the next morning. By the time I finish that exercise, I have three or four pages of handwritten notes. Also, I have one other thing—an emerging outline that has come out of that text. I have my outline before I ever consult any of the commentaries—that's the second stage, I go to the commentaries. In my experience, if you go to the commentaries first, it stifles your creativity because you are fixed on what someone else has said rather than a spontaneous reaction of your own. I think you ought to go to the text with as clear a mind and spirit as you possibly can. I don't want someone else to force their vocabulary on me and my responsibilities.

Interviewer: Your sermons shift from inductive to deductive reasoning and vice versa. Is that a conscious methodology or a formalized philosophy of preaching?

Harrington: It is all of that. I combine both modes of reasoning. Actually, I have a full manuscript in the pulpit when I preach. I think the preacher should discipline himself to write out a full manuscript. I have in that manuscript more material than I can preach in the time allotted, and there is something creative in the moment of delivery where you've got to delete some material. It's in that creative tension that you respond to the needs of the people who are before you. That tension gives my preaching whatever vitality it has.

Interviewer: You give a great deal of attention to sermon titles. How do you develop these titles, and how do they function in the context of a preaching schedule?

Harrington: I think one of the most crucial issues is titles. It's amazing—I get a lot of church bulletins. What astounds me is the number of church bulletins in which no sermon title is announced. That is a lost opportunity! I announce my sermon topics six months in advance; I could announce them a year in advance! I really work on that and I think that's a very important opportunity.

Interviewer: Your ministry at Peachtree has seen the church grow to an incredible size and influence. To what degree has preaching been the mainstay of your ministry?

Harrington: I think it's been at the heart of everything we have done. That is not to say that I am the chief cause of it. You know, great people encourage great preaching. Many people say the preacher makes the church, but the very opposite of that is true. The church makes the preacher. I have been encouraged immensely by the members of this church to go into the pulpit and preach what God has laid on my heart. I have never had anyone suggest that I do otherwise, and the reason for that, I think, is because the prophetic and the pastoral must go together.

When I stand to preach it's within this family of faith in which we love each other. Together we have known happiness and heartbreak, success and sadness, triumph and tragedy; and if you can't talk about the things that are vital in this context, then where in God's name *can* you talk about them? I think the prophetic and the pastoral always go together.

Interviewer: You are the only preacher in Atlanta listed in the 100 Most Influential People published in *Atlanta Business Weekly*. To what degree does your role as a public preacher inform your ministry here?

Harrington: It's interesting. Several people called me about that and several people mailed the article to me. That's the second or third time I've been in such a list. I have thought about that a great deal and I think that whatever influence I have, it is a product of trying to be a faithful pastor to my people and a faithful witness for Jesus Christ. The influence that I have is because of the possibility that I may impact the people who sit in this church week after week after week, and through them, impact this city. You see, the reality is that if I can influence the people who sit in the pews of this church to walk closer to Jesus Christ, this church can have a role in shaping the destiny of this city. That is both a great opportunity and a great responsibility.

Interviewer: How do you construct your worship services around the preaching event?

Harrington: Worship here is designed to be celebrative. We meet every Sunday to celebrate the resurrection of Jesus Christ. Worship is celebrative in nature and always invitational. It begins with an invitation and ends with an invitation, so that worship is uplifting and joyous. We change certain elements in the worship service so that it does not become a matter of rote that we just routinely go through each service. There may be a creed in the service one Sunday, and the next Sunday there may be a confession for sin and assurance of pardon, a responsive reading, or a litany. There should be a creative tension operative there.

Interviewer: You have a very large congregation, but you seem to have a very strong personal connection with them.

Harrington: When I stand up to preach, I don't look out at a mass, I look out at individuals. I look over there and I see a couple that I married five years ago and their two boys. I look over there and I see a young couple who are engaged, or I see a young man home from college, or a young woman who just finished her medical training. I watched those people grow up, you see. I've been here now over twenty years. I've married many people whom I had confirmed into the membership of this church—and I'm now baptizing their babies. It's all like a great family to me and I want to see them each Sunday.

Interviewer: How much is your length of tenure here related to the effectiveness of your ministry?

Harrington: It's a part of it. You become a trusted individual, which is a tremendous responsibility. I've had people quote back to me things I said five years ago. That'll cause you to stay

> *The reality is that if I can influence the people who sit in the pews of this church to walk closer to Jesus Christ, this church can have a role in shaping the destiny of this city.*

on your knees! That's certainly a part of it. I have a theory that there are no strong churches in the urban environment, and it may be true in any environment where there is not a history of long pastorates. This church is seventy-two years old this year, and it's had five pastors. I'm the only one still alive, but two of us in the five have served about fifty-four years.

It's a continuity factor. Continuity is extremely important. This congregation knows that on forty-five to forty-eight Sundays a year, I'm going to be in this service at least twice every Sunday. Over a period of years, you build a great setting for the proclamation of the Good News.

Interviewer: I note the effectiveness of your Southern rhetorical style in your preaching. How did you learn to preach?

Harrington: I knew I was going to be a minister before I was a senior in high school. My early ambition was to be a lawyer and to run for governor of South Carolina. So early on as a school student, I began to enter speaking contests and debate competitions. If you're going to be a political figure, you need to be able to think on your feet and to articulate what your convictions are. When I look back, I can see the hand of God in all that. An individual's style must be authentic to who that individual is. One of the things people say to me is: "Oh, you're not any different in person than you are in the pulpit." That's very important. It always astounds me somewhat. Why wouldn't I be the same person? I think if you develop some sort of a phony stained-glass personality it doesn't work . . . at least it won't work for long.

Interviewer: At the end of the twentieth century, you hear the suggestion that preaching is passé, yet there is not a church of any size which does not feature a strong preaching ministry. On the one hand, we see a renaissance of preaching, and yet other sectors of the church have given up on it. What is your message to the church about the importance of preaching?

Harrington: I will come back to where I began—preaching is the central task of the minister. My own judgment is that we are going to move into a tremendous era of renewal in preaching. I have on my desk right now five folders in which are several letters from churches asking me to recommend them a minister. And those churches range in membership from about 350 to 3,800. All of them have one central issue—recommend someone who is an effective preacher. I think if you can create a caring environment in an uplifting worship environment, and have standing at the center of that a person who can articulate the truth of God in relevant terminology, you would be hard-pressed to have a building big enough to hold the people.

You have to constantly maintain that time for preparation, and if ministers ever get to the point where they are relying on what they did five years ago, they will dry up spiritually. We must be constantly digging and grappling with the central questions, because that's what causes us to grow. In our growth, we can help our people grow.

July/August 1992

6

THE MEDIA WILL CHALLENGE PREACHERS TO EXCELLENCE

David Allen Hubbard

As president of Fuller Theological Seminary in Pasadena, California, for three decades, David Allen Hubbard was involved in the training of hundreds of evangelical preachers. Now retired, he is a popular preacher and lecturer, and is the author of a large number of books and articles. Along with many other places of leadership within the evangelical world, Dr. Hubbard also serves as a contributing editor of *Preaching* magazine.

Interviewer: As president at Fuller Seminary, you're involved in training future ministers. How do you think today's seminarians view preaching as part of their ministerial role?

Hubbard: I think that preaching is as crucial in the minds of today's seminarians as it has been anytime during my ministry. I first seriously started thinking about preaching in college, so

I've had forty years of looking at the situation and learning something about students.

I look back at my own student days, and then I look back at what the feelings were when I first came to Fuller as president in 1963. Then there was a lot more uncertainty about preaching and the role of the local church; whether we should be in dialogue and whether the sermon was as central to the worship and nurture of the church as tradition had made it.

I would say that for the past five years, probably, the students at Fuller have more than returned to where we were in the early days, with a strong emphasis on preaching, and they are much more deeply into it themselves than would have been true of our students in the '60s.

Interviewer: In the '60s there was a move toward social activism. Do you see more of a balance today or do you see simply a shift away from an emphasis on social activism?

Hubbard: I think balance is probably the right word. I do see this as a balanced generation. I think the balance between learning and piety, the balance between preaching and other forms of ministry, and the balance between evangelism and social action are very healthy. I don't think there is any day in the life of any institution that I have been a part of that was better balanced than today's student is. I think there is a lot of concern for Scripture, a lot of concern for preaching of Scripture—how you do it—but also a lot of concern for the artistry, the impact of it.

In our situation, part of the renewal of this has been brought by our women students. For the past two or three years, I would say they have probably drawn the lion's share of the prizes. I mean, we have some very remarkable women preachers. We have a scholarship program that a friend of the seminary has set up that enables our top graduates in preaching to spend a year overseas. It's a nine-thousand-dollar prize, and I think that more than half of the winners in the last three years have been women.

Interviewer: What do you think is the future of female students once they leave the seminary setting and try and move into the churches? What kind of response are they going to have?

Hubbard: It will depend on where the church tradition is that they are a part of. If they are Roman Catholic, they are going to be very articulate nuns, at least probably for our lifetime. In the denominations that have been very open in the last twenty-five years—United Church of Christ, United Presbyterian, American Baptist, of course a number of the Pentecostal denominations—I think they will do very well at the preaching level.

Where they will have more difficulty is in being pastors of multiple-staff churches. I think it is true, still, that in the whole United Presbyterian denomination, which has literally hundreds and hundreds of ordained women, there is not one of them holding a position as senior pastor in a multiple-staff church. So the difficulty will be at the point of the running of a large organization.

Now those large churches will very often have a very effective woman as an associate pastor who will lead in worship and preach regularly. I know numbers of women in those churches who just are marvelous in public presence and lead worship with joy. A congregation is lifted by the way these women lead the congregation in worship. When they are called to preach maybe once a month or while the senior pastor is on vacation, they do extraordinarily well.

On the managerial side—the full leadership of working with a session, and all of that—it is similar to the situation in the school system. You have lots of women in the school systems who are assistant superintendents for curriculum and for teacher training. You don't have many school districts in the nation where the superintendent of schools, working with the board directly, is a woman. I was on the state board of education in California about a dozen years ago. There were only about two or three women out of about a thousand school districts—and you know how many bright assistant superintendents there were. But the school board wasn't ready to trust the entire governance of the district to a woman. I think administrative leadership for women is going to take a little while longer, but I do think that many churches that have not been used to hearing women preach will get used to that and understand how effective a communicator a woman can be.

So it is taking time, but I would say in Methodist churches where bishops have the power to make things happen a little more, and in Presbyterian churches where they have worked hard to bring in women, that women are being very well received. I could take you to some places where our graduates preach and do incredibly well. You just don't want to be second speaker on the program after them. They are marvelous communicators.

Interviewer: What place do you think preaching should have within a seminary curriculum?

Hubbard: Preaching ought to be on everybody's mind in a seminary curriculum. I think that those of us who teach in biblical studies, historical studies, dogmatics, and so forth, need to have at least half an eye on the ministry of the local church and on the preaching ministry as we teach. On the other hand, the crew in preaching needs to be a quality crew, needs to know how to reach back into those other disciplines and make a bridge. Integration unto preaching, I suppose, would be the catchphrase that I would use for that.

One model that is probably a bit of caricature, but that has existed in certain seminaries, is that the biblical and theological people do their stuff and hand it to the student, and then the homiletics people do their stuff in terms of techniques of sermon preparation and all of that and hand it to the student, and the student has been forced to do the integrating. Now we are at the point where we all integrate. In whatever we do in the curriculum, we are looking at the ministry of the church as we do it, and particularly, I would say, at preaching and worship.

It's a labor-intensive task. It's like coaching quarterbacks or tight ends or anything like that. You can't do it by the hundreds, you can only do it by the few. It takes a lot of people to do it. The whole seminary has to believe that preaching is central. As I teach Old Testament—how to interpret the text—I have to give them some help as to how I get to the sermon from the text, and not just teach them the text. At least I need to do some modeling about the application of that text in pastoral ministry, counseling, administration, and so forth, but particularly how I go from text to sermon.

Interviewer: How do you help the pastor who is out on the field now without that kind of training?

Hubbard: I think maybe two or three things there. One would be the use of tapes and a very conscious analysis of what some of the people that he would most admire, or that have proven most effective, are doing on tapes. I think he needs to listen. I think that listening to sermons probably is a little more authentic way to catch the spirit of them than reading is, even though we want to read sermons. But a sermon always has to have that other dimension. We don't stand up in the pulpit and hand out the text and have twenty-five minutes of silence while everybody reads it.

He can also establish a relationship with a preacher that he admires, being vulnerable enough, weak enough, and open enough to say to the person, "I would be very interested in any help that you could give me if I could meet with you occasionally. Would you, for instance, be willing to talk with me a little about how you do it? Would you be willing to share with me the two or three books that have helped you most?" So you establish a tutorial or mentoring relationship with someone.

I know people that have formed groups to work together on things, covenant groups that work together to help each other. Eugene Peterson is at Christ the King Presbyterian Church in Bel Air, Maryland. One of the things that he has done every week for many years is to hold a Bible study with a number of his fellow pastors and do the exegesis with them that would provide some of the background for preaching. That's a little more formal setup where many of them preach from the lectionary, which would be a little different from what we as Baptists usually do.

He will swat up the lectionary passage or passages every week and then I think the Episcopal pastor, the Lutheran pastor, and some friends meet with him and they have fellowship. There is sharing and they talk about their preaching, but Gene leads them in a Bible study and helps them with their exegesis. It is a great gift to the community when you think that in all those churches they have gone a little more deeply into the Scripture under his leadership than they would without that.

I am sure that there would also be, in a community, the possibility of getting four or five pastors in a kind of covenant commitment who, again, willing to be vulnerable, would be willing to bring in a sermon on a rotating basis, maybe one each month. They would listen to the sermon together and then talk about what they like, what they thought was strong, and so forth. There can be a lot of that peer coaching and sharing if people will give it some priority.

Interviewer: Is it really possible to teach a person to preach?

Hubbard: Sure. Teaching the person to study well and to know what to look for in the text and how to handle the text is a key. I think there is a natural fluency that some people have that others don't. But I think there are a lot of ways to compensate for lack of fluency, like giving a person practice in being a good manuscript preacher or a good preacher from extensive notes; there is a good bit of help there and the person doesn't have to ad-lib.

I think ideally a journeyman preacher needs to be able to ad-lib, needs to be able to preach from memory, needs to be able to preach from notes, and needs to be able to preach well from a manuscript. I personally have disciplined myself intentionally through the years to do all of those and combinations of them, because I have not wanted to be locked into any one style of preaching. But people who don't have a natural gift of gab, by very thoughtful preparation, choosing their illustrations well, planning and carefully outlining, knowing how to build to a climax, knowing when to quit, they could do some ad-libbing.

There is a tremendous amount that can be learned. I have seen some of my colleagues who were good preachers ten years ago become great preachers by working at it. They have just disciplined themselves to work at it. In the long run, it can be a bit of a disadvantage to be a natural preacher, because I think the people who are, especially in our free church tradition, tend to rest on that. I know people whom you can hear once and then hear them ten years later and they wouldn't sound any different. A natural preacher, unless he really works at it, is going to be as good at the beginning as he is at the end; he needs to develop those gifts. It's like a person who can play the piano well by ear in the key of F. They transpose everything into the key of F and ten years later they're still playing in the key of F and they're still doing the same kind of stuff. They haven't studied it; they haven't worked at it.

One of the advantages that comes from *not* being a naturally fluent or articulate preacher is that you keep forcing yourself to grow. You maintain a self-criticism that asks every time after you make a presentation, "How could I have done that better?"

If you can get a natural talent really disciplined by someone who will work his tail off to be a good communicator, then you've got the stuff of which greatness is made.

Interviewer: What part does preaching play in your own personal ministry?

Hubbard: It has played different parts in different eras in my life. When I was a college teacher, I did a lot of conference ministry—young people's conferences, campus missions, and things like that. Preaching was a key part of that. For a period of time when I was a college teacher, I preached regularly in a church that I helped to found until they were able to get large enough to afford a full-time minister; it was an Evangelical Covenant church in Santa Barbara where my son-in-law and daughter attend. I preached three times a week for a couple of years in that situation.

Two things give me the greatest delight in a preaching ministry. One is to preach to our own students, as I try to do about four or five times a year in chapel. Usually the first chapel of each term I preach and then occasionally other times in between. I really enjoy preaching to preachers. I also enjoy talking about preaching. I think if I didn't hold a chair in Old Testament I would love to have a chair in homiletics, because I really enjoy teaching preaching.

I was on the radio virtually every week from 1969 to 1980. That was a great time for me. I had almost a dozen years on *The Joyful Sound* radio broadcast, which carried on the Old-Fashioned Revival Hour ministry under a different name. It was very difficult and very demanding, because I was preparing forty-some new sermons a year, just as a working clergyperson does, and still carrying on all the administrative and teaching responsibilities at the seminary. That was a high-demand time. Yet it was very rewarding and very challenging to be into the Word every week like that with new ideas and thoughts and then the responsibility of asking, How do I make it clear? How can I make it sing? How can I make it live? That kind of exercise in my life was very important and that was a very formative time for me.

Interviewer: What kind of process do you go through yourself when you are preparing a sermon?

Hubbard: Unless it's a special event, like a funeral, I try to plan what I do in series. I try to plan a whole year's preaching a year ahead; my friends who I think do the best in preaching do that. I have friends who take a whole month in the summer as

> *One of the advantages that comes from not being a naturally fluent or articulate preacher is that you keep forcing yourself to grow.*

part of their study leave. They take vacation, that's one thing, but then they take a month away from the church and do the basic planning, plotting, outlining, thinking, and praying about what the emphasis in their preaching and in the congregation needs to be.

I do think that if there is any fault that we fall into as pastors, it's letting the ball play us—reacting to what is going on, and therefore getting caught with short lead time. I know some people who never work more than about a month ahead of time. I suppose there are some people who work only about a week or two ahead of time. I have to say that's hard work. I also feel that it is a waste of energy, because nobody can live that way without some anxiety, and any energy that goes into anxiety ought to go into planning.

I would start by planning long in advance, and maybe that includes several series of different lengths, with maybe a Thanksgiving sermon, a short series for Christmas, and a short series for Lent leading up to Easter. I'm not talking about preaching on the same thing all year, although I have friends who just about do that. They'll take a biblical book and stay in it all year. I would plan a series—by that I mean setting up the topics, choosing the

texts, the individual sermons. I would try in that planning se-
quence, then, to prepare a summary of each of those. What do
I want to say from that text, basically? That's about one paragraph, two typed inches. Do that months ahead.

Planning ahead has several advantages: First, your choir director can look at anthems and solos. This way you can prepare better for worship and integrate music and liturgy. Second, you can
publicize what's coming up as a way of getting the congregation
involved; they are anticipating it. The series you are giving at the
time may be more specialized, and some people may not feel that
they are as touched or helped by that. So you tell them that the
next thing coming is going to be on family life or prayer or how
to relate your Christian faith to your work or whatever it is. They
will plug in; they will say, "Hey, I can hardly wait for that. I will
be glad when he's going to be on that." So there is anticipation
that has developed.

Another thing that happens when we plan ahead is that our
unconscious starts to work on those areas. We make connections
between things we read, stories we hear, television programs we
watch, a movie we see, whatever it is, and we begin to think about
illustrations. We might have a system where we clip out a page
from *Time* magazine because it's got an article that relates to our
series, or we write a note about a story that we've read, or we
photocopy a page in a book that's going to relate to our topic
and stick it in a folder. I keep a folder. When I know what I'm
going to preach on for a series, I have a folder in a cabinet in my
desk, and anything that I hit that relates to anything that's coming up gets tucked in there. I don't have to have tricky filing systems and I don't try to collect illustrations in a vacuum. I collect illustrations related to what I know I am going to have to do.
But if I know my series six months in advance, a year in advance,
I've got a lot of time to start to put that together.

One of the hardest things that you have when you preach is to
come down to the preparation of the sermon and say, "How do
I illustrate that?" Then you find you're making up illustrations
or stealing or cheating or using old illustrations again. But if
you've thought about it a long time, your mind will signal you
when you encounter a good illustration.

Another thing preparing that far ahead does is that you don't have to think at all about what topic you are going to speak on. You've decided that earlier. You don't argue with yourself and thumb through the New Testament and look at four or five areas, and say, "Well, which is better for the congregation for two weeks from today? Is it better to do this or that?" All of that is avoided.

What you do is execute. You have already laid the plan, and now you execute the plan. You have no energy that goes into indecisiveness. If you're indecisive, you can sit there for a couple of hours and just waste those two hours. During those two

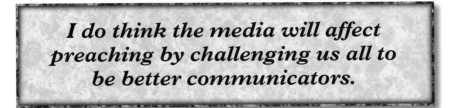

I do think the media will affect preaching by challenging us all to be better communicators.

hours you could have outlined half the sermon. So you've got the topic settled well in advance and you've got a summary of what you think you want to say. That summary becomes the start of your outline and you waste no time in planning.

Once I have decided on those topics way ahead and prepared those short summaries, there comes the time when I have to execute. Then I will spend a lot of time in the text itself. I will look at the Greek. I will look at the technical commentaries. Usually I will do that after I have done a good bit of spade work on the text myself, because I really want to bring my own judgment to it first and then check that judgment and fill it out by my reading. So I would go to the text first, get as good a grasp of it as I can, and then backfill that. You want to be fair to the text and the state of your understanding of the text.

Next, I take one sheet of paper for each sermon. On that sheet I list the topic, text, theme (the one thing that I want to try to say that I think the text is teaching us), introduction, and conclusion. I have a kind of standardized photocopied sheet for this with space for the introduction and space for the conclusion. It has four roman numerals for the points. I almost always will preach between two and four points. I try not to get into a fifth; five points is a lot to carry forward.

Then that page is divided into three columns vertically. On the left-hand side of the page is the outline of the sermon where those four points are. In the middle of the page is a heading that I call "seed thoughts." The right-hand column is for illustrations. I do that because I want the layout of the sermon before me where I can look at the whole thing at once; you do not prepare a sermon systematically, the way you might prepare an outline for an essay. Your mind doesn't work one, two, three. Your mind jumps and it flashes you various signals. Sometimes you will get the closing line of the sermon before you get anything else. If you get that closing line, write it down. I don't try to remember it, because I may get interrupted; the older you get the harder it is to recall.

Then I keep looking at the text, working up and down through it, trying to break it down. What are its natural points? What is it trying to say? What does the text unpack? I put my jottings in the column that I call seed thoughts. Sometimes they come out balanced expressions or summaries of those points and you can go almost from there right to the outline. Sometimes it is just thoughts and ideas that you think that the writer is dealing with.

Then I would go from there, after the seed thoughts, to try to shape the outline. I just take my first jottings from the seed thoughts section for the outline. While you are doing that, you may get an illustration for point two. Or you may think of the lead line for the introduction. You write it all down, because you've got the space for it. I try to get that sheet about filled with seed thoughts, some ideas of illustrations for each point, and the outline's basic points and subpoints. You have to go with points and subpoints—you can't go subpoints of your subpoints very well. My typical form would be I, II, III (a three-point sermon), with subpoints A and B, maybe A, B, C, but probably not more than that under each of those main points. So I am carrying through somewhere between six and nine total points—three main points and not more than three subpoints under each of those.

I get those outline points written out and make sure they are stylistically balanced. When I've got that, depending on what I'm going to do with it, I will either write notes on half sheets of paper or on index cards. I use cards like that quite often to preach

> *In congregational life, the media will stimulate us to have a more lively experience of fellowship in worship.*

from; they are stiff enough so that they won't blow around or fold over on me. If I am going to do the sermon on the radio, or if it's something that I might later want to do as a book, then I will sit down and write out the whole thing. Once I have that basic outline, then I can do an average sermon in between three and four hours.

I have thought about the sermon a lot by the time I get to that point. I have spent most of my adult life doing biblical exegesis. I have had a lot of preparation. I have had that topic on my mind maybe for a year. So there is a lot of inner preparation. You cannot do that in three or four hours if you start cold. But one of the advantages of giving yourself a long lead time is your unconscious works, literally preparing you to deliver that sermon for months.

The other advantage of doing all of that preparation is what I hinted at when I said you might publish it. If you preach in series and you organize yourself that well, the amount of time it takes to write that is very little. Then you can end up with a manuscript that can be a chapter in a book. You have just opened up the possibility of a much wider audience, even if all you do is just circulate that in your congregation. If they say, "Oh, that really moved me." You say, "Okay, next Sunday in the narthex there will be typed copies of the sermon I gave the week before." People can take them home, mark them, share them with friends. You can probably very easily triple or quadruple the distribution and effectiveness. Once you are doing that much homework, to be able to put that little in it to make it available is the key.

Interviewer: Do you see any changes coming in preaching in the next few years? How will media affect it?

Hubbard: I do think the media will affect preaching by challenging us all to be better communicators. There is more available to committed Christians. If I am going to talk about personal problems and the application of Christian faith, and they're all going to go off to the other church to see Swindoll on tape, that is a challenge to me to do better.

Ruth and I watch Lloyd Ogilvie most of the time on Sunday morning at eight o'clock before we go off to our First Baptist Church. One of America's great preachers is available to us while we are sipping our second cup of coffee in the morning. That's just got to mean that we have to take preaching in the congregation more seriously, because the best people in the land are instantly available to us.

I do think media will make available a wider dissemination of our own ministries. I mean, for years people have taken audio tapes off to the shut-ins and so forth. There's no reason now why any congregation can't take videotapes. Videotape the service. Let the people in the convalescent home and the shut-ins hear the choir, see the sermon. The people who feel cut off from the church can see it and experience it in their own rooms, nursing homes, or whatever in a way that was not available before.

In congregational life, the media will stimulate us to have a more lively experience of fellowship in worship. That is the thing we can offer most in contrast to the media, where you are there in isolation and you are just watching a performance. If a Sunday morning service is just another example of sitting there in isolation because you don't sense any community and you're not really into the service, you are a spectator. I do think that a lot of our Sunday services are performance oriented, not participation oriented. What I would like to see is a combination of Baptist preaching and Episcopal liturgy—getting the congregation going in prayer and responses and Scripture readings and all of that kind of thing.

In our free church tradition, particularly as Baptists, we talk of the priesthood of believers, and we "non-priest" every believer in church. They don't go there as priests. They go there as spectators. The pastor and the choir do the whole thing, and then we say, "Now, you are priests." We don't give them very much opportunity to offer their sacrifices of praise to God at all. If you look at the average service, there may be a responsive reading, the singing of a couple of hymns, but that congregation is pretty passive except for listening. I think we are denying our own theology by the way we conduct our worship.

With alternative sermons and first-class music available at home, unless something goes on in the life of the congregation, we end up just whipping people into coming to church by guilt. They're not coming because they really feel like this is an indispensable experience for them. They don't get the sense of joy, of giving to God their worship and praise. And they don't always have the sense of experiencing the unity of the body of Christ and the gifts of the other members of the congregation helping nurture them. They get that out of Bible study groups some, and they get that out of some Sunday school groups, and so forth. I would say it's not just in the area of preaching, but it's in the area of the total experience of worship and fellowship that we need to do the most improving, and in a sense, the media represents the greatest threat to us.

September/October 1986

7

PREACHING WITH A PROPHETIC EDGE

John A. Huffman Jr.

One of the Presbyterian church's outstanding contemporary preachers is John A. Huffman Jr., now pastor of St. Andrews Presbyterian Church in Newport Beach, California. A graduate of Princeton Theological Seminary, Huffman served as a young minister on the staff of Marble Collegiate Church with Norman Vincent Peale. He served as associate pastor of First Presbyterian Church in Tulsa, Oklahoma, then moved to the pastorate of Key Biscayne Presbyterian Church in Key Biscayne, Florida. Huffman became pastor of the historic First Presbyterian Church in Pittsburgh, Pennsylvania, prior to coming to Newport Beach.

Active as a leader in a variety of evangelical causes, Huffman is also a contributing editor of *Preaching* magazine.

Interviewer: You have served churches coast-to-coast in a variety of settings—from Key Biscayne to the industrial city of Pittsburgh, and now Newport Beach, which seems like something of a resort setting.

Huffman: I am in what looks like a resort area, but isn't. It is a hardworking community. This is really a residential, work-type atmosphere. The community of Key Biscayne had a pleasure ethic, while Pittsburgh had a work ethic. I am now in a work ethic and pleasure ethic environment; it may look like a resort, but to the people who live here, it isn't. You can't live here without really working hard. They come from all over and move very fast, but it's not a resort like Florida was.

Interviewer: As you've moved from one type or kind of community to another, how would you say your preaching has changed?

Huffman: I am not sure that my style or content has really changed. What has changed is my reading of the culture and the kind of language I speak. In each situation, I have had to "go native" fast and learn to understand the local dialect.

Each time I've moved to a new area I've had to do two things: First, being sure that nothing is lost in terms of the gospel, I compromise like crazy to try to speak the local language, to try to understand the culture and speak the language the people speak. Then I try to speak to that culture in terms of the prophetic word.

For example, I followed Ben Haden in Key Biscayne, and I felt they wanted me to be very evangelistic. I formalized the style, put a robe on, and put the pulpit back in the sanctuary. There were northerners coming down who were visiting and might have been turned off by the informal type of environment. We built a very strong attendance from visitors from the north and I preached evangelistically, but in a more formal, nonverbal style of worship setting. By that I don't mean high church—I just mean it looked less like a Southern Baptist church than it had with Ben's style. In the process, I probably lost some of the Southern Baptist-type people because of my image, but we very carefully targeted those northerners.

When I moved to Pittsburgh, I went into a very evangelical preaching style. At First Presbyterian, I followed Robert Lamont, and the congregation was very well trained in cognitive thought, theology, and biblical preaching. I tried to learn the language of that ministry, and I think I adapted myself to their environment. What I did then was to introduce relational preaching.

My style is what I call biblical, life-situation preaching. I am not just a relational preacher and I'm not just an expository preacher; I try to combine both elements. In that environment, I felt they needed a lot of preaching on relationships.

In Pittsburgh, I did a series for eight weeks on family relationships that became somewhat controversial in the church because they had not had that kind of preaching before. Our printed sermon list grew from three hundred to three thousand in eight weeks, yet our attendance in church dropped about 15 percent during that time. I had not quite understood the dynamics of singleness in that congregation. To the people who were not married, especially the older singles, all the talk about spouses and children was alienating.

Then I came here into an environment that was not distinctly labeled. It was not labeled an evangelical church, as the previous churches I had served were, and here there was a love for relational preaching. I felt I was called to preach from the Book of Romans, and I spent some forty weeks in the Book of Romans early in my ministry. It almost broke my back and almost broke the back of the people, but it was what really made the ministry here in the early years. That's because I was not just learning the local environment, I was trying to establish a doctrinal base.

It's not that I didn't preach the same kind of sermons in both places. I did, but the emphasis was to swim against the stream a little bit. Don't just do what comes naturally—you need to be able to bring a new dimension to that environment.

Interviewer: You talked about "going native" in each area—dealing with the particular culture in that church without sacrificing the message. Would you say that involved primarily the particular way you use language? What other elements could be involved?

Huffman: Well, it involves everything. It involves the total being of a pastor. This was driven home when Anne and I were with some Bible translators in the Solomon Islands. We were brought there to spend ten days with these twenty-five translators who were ministering in an area equivalent to Los Angeles to Phoenix to San Francisco and back to Denver—that big an area to service—with some seventy languages.

Now I am not a good language student for some reason. I was not gifted with that. My grandfather was a translator and a scholar, but that does not come naturally for me. I have always felt somewhat intimidated by translators, and there I was doing Bible teaching in the morning while my wife, who is a psychotherapist, was doing some relational things in the afternoon.

We sat through all of their sessions. These people get together once every two years—they deal with their translation problems, with what's going on in their computers, and they talk to you about what you do in a culture where you are trying to translate Jesus as the Good Shepherd and there are no sheep! They got into this and I began realizing that that is the way it is in Newport Beach.

The reality is that I am a translator. I could take you over to Calvary Chapel, or one of the small churches in the area, and every one of these people speaks a little bit different language. Chuck Smith, whom I love very much, speaks a language of the working class, primarily blue-collar. He is sort of a father figure

> *The reality is that I am a translator. That means immersing myself in what they read, do, and think, yet trying to bring to it a prophetic edge.*

to the whole generation who came up in the tough time of the late '60s. In the Newport Beach area, I see all the way from the yuppie couple to the fast-moving single, so the language I speak is primarily in the thirty-eight to seventy-five age bracket—people who are well established and are at a mature point of their lives. I have to speak a language they can relate to. That means immersing myself in what they read, do, and think, yet trying to bring to it a prophetic edge.

Interviewer: As you try to immerse yourself in the culture of your people, how does that affect your reading program? Are there some particular kinds of literature or publications that you try to read?

Huffman: I take the concept that my preaching has to be done with the Bible in one hand and the *New York Times* in the other—although in this culture it's the *Los Angeles Times* and *Time* magazine. I do get the Sunday *New York Times.* I am a news junkie, and this is an information environment here, so I really try to stay on top of what is going on in the world. Our people travel all over the place and are very much alert to what goes on, so I really keep up with the news journals. I also read publications such as *Christianity Today* and *Christian Century* so that I know what is going on in the world of thought and what is happening in the religious world.

In addition to that, my real interest is in history and biography. On vacation, I normally take two or three biographies with me. I find out a lot about life through biography, so that's basically my reading. I don't watch as much television as I should or go to movies as much as I should. I find myself not particularly caring about television, yet I have to really discipline myself periodically to watch—just to know what my people are exposed to. My kids keep me up on those things.

Interviewer: Are there particular people in the area of homiletics who have influenced you?

Huffman: I don't approach homiletics in a formal textbook approach per se. But early on in my ministry, when I realized that I was going into the ministry, I set some goals. I wanted to have some of the power and heart for the Lord in terms of evangelism like Billy Graham, some of the academic responsibility in terms of my study and preparation of someone like Harold Ockenga, the down-to-earth quality of Norman Vincent Peale. Phillips Brooks is another example—I used his Yale Lectures on Preaching as a basis for my doctoral thesis.

Interviewer: One of the major ways many ministers have come to know your ministry is through your sermons as they are published and distributed in booklet form. How many of these are mailed?

Huffman: There are about five thousand sent each week, to fifty states and three foreign countries. There is no charge for

them—they are free, though if a person wants to give a donation, that is fine.

Interviewer: As I receive those sermons regularly and follow
your preaching, it seems you do a lot of sermon series. How
much of your preaching schedule is filled by series?

Huffman: When I started out my ministry in Florida, I don't
think I did any series that I can remember. What I did preach was
out of my devotional life. I would read through the Bible, and every
time I hit a verse that spoke to me, I would take out a sheet of paper
and write down the topic and what it meant to me. I must have
squirreled away four hundred or five hundred of those sheets—still
untouched, but my preaching emerged out of that. Then I realized
the danger of that approach was that I was preaching only on the
things that were hitting me, and that was purely topical preaching.

I did some short series on the family when I got to Pittsburgh,
and realized that I wanted to deepen that in terms of some word
studies occasionally. In this church, I am probably half of the
time in series, maybe a little bit more than that. A series can be
anything from three to five weeks up to a better part of the year.
Last spring I asked our people what topics they would like their
pastor to address—abortion, authority, money, evolution, suffering—and I did a series on them in the fall, what the Bible says
and doesn't say about these topics.

The thing I want to be sure of is that I don't just jump around
in topics. I have preached eighteen messages about Joshua. The
people are very helpful to me in planning for a series.

Interviewer: Do you find particular benefits that make you
enjoy doing series preaching?

Huffman: I think what I get out of a series is the opportunity
to take people a little bit deeper in Scripture. If I had only six
more weeks to preach, I would not do a series. I would preach
on the resurrection and other definitive topics of biblical faith.
If you preach topically for fifty years, the danger is that you will
lose some of the richness and depth that are possible in a series.

Interviewer: Tell us a bit about the process you use in planning your own preaching.

Huffman: I try to get away in the summer and plan my
preaching for the year. Some pastors may actually set up their

topics for a year, though I think few of us get as much done in the summer as we would like people to think we do. In the summer, I at least try to see my way through the Advent season as to where I am going; then I basically try to stay about three months ahead in terms of my topics.

I really don't begin preparing a specific sermon until the week before the Sunday I preach. I am not suggesting that is the way to preach, but it is a lot better than not starting until Saturday afternoon, which I know many people do! By six o'clock Friday evening, I try to have my sermon complete; if I can't meet that deadline, then on a few occasions I finish it on Saturday morning and my secretary will come in and type it up. But I don't use a manuscript at all while I am preaching.

During the week, I do sit down with a piece of paper and the Bible and pretend that I am writing a topic for a campus life group. I make a thesis statement based on the Scripture passage. I determine what central thrust is there and what comes out of

> *If I had only six more weeks to preach, I would not do a series. I would preach on the resurrection.*

that passage to me. I draw a conclusion—what I would say on the basis of just a very brief encounter with the text; then I put that away and I begin to study. I will begin to scribble notes from my reading; if it involves a word study I will have a sheet or two on those studies.

Then I will file all that until Thursday, which is my general review day. I sometimes play golf on Thursday, but what I really try to do is to feel no pressure. I have some ideas of what others have said on this passage and thoughts of what I can say on it. Then I just shift my mind into neutral and enjoy reading *Time* magazine or *Psychology Today;* I let things flow. I may read some church history. I keep books laying around all the time.

Friday morning is the countdown. I make no appointments and I hope to have all of my writing outline done by then. Then I dictate in a machine to be given to my secretary; I find I save myself about 50 percent of the time it would take to sit at a computer or typewriter to do it. With dictation, I also orally color it. Then my secretary types this up.

I don't look at it through the day on Saturday. Late in the day, I sit down and take that manuscript and I do my preaching outline with topic and the text. I fold it in half and that is what I memorize. Saturday night I spend a little time with the family and I read the sermon over a couple of times trying to memorize the outline.

Sunday morning I get up and read the *New York Times* and the *Los Angeles Times,* do my devotions, then mentally try to see the outline. It helps in remembering it by writing it down. I read over the manuscript several times and say, "Lord, I have done my homework—now it is up to you." I eat breakfast, do my exercises, shave and shower, then read over my outline and keep it with me.

Interviewer: Do you try to memorize that outline or particular sections of it?

Huffman: No. In the eighth grade I had a course in literature where I had to memorize the "Midnight Ride of Paul Revere." I blanked out about a third of the way through, and I vowed then I would never memorize and be dependent only on my memory. I decided early on some people are gifted with word color and I admire them, but I need to look my listener right in the eye, not through a manuscript. I take a little bit longer than I would if I was reading or memorizing it, but I know that I couldn't memorize it. I want people to look at me just like I am looking at them—in the eyes. I want that type of contact.

Interviewer: How long have you used that method of delivery?

Huffman: Right from the beginning. When I was in New York, I watched Peale do this with a formula approach. I am a biblical preacher—my central thrust is on the message: It depends on the text of Scripture. I like things to be down-to-earth, to get the sermon right out there to the people—to just speak directly to them.

Interviewer: I know that you serve on the board of trustees of Gordon-Conwell Divinity School, and have had a good bit of contact with other colleges and seminaries. How do you think seminaries and colleges are doing in preparing young ministers for the preaching task?

Huffman: I think that we are doing a wonderful job of teaching the content, in terms of theology or church history. I don't know how well we are doing in terms of training people to preach. In fact, one of the complaints I increasingly hear is that students learn good tools, but not necessarily the right practice.

I was blessed to be at Princeton, learning under superb people. They are harder to find today. Most people who are gifted preachers want to preach—they aren't in the classroom reading student sermons and working with the students. I am talking about denominational and nondenominational schools. It differs from seminary to seminary.

It's awfully hard to learn to preach at a seminary, anyway. But it is very important to young persons going into a preaching ministry to try to write a manuscript a week. Don't be tied to that manuscript, but by writing and putting your words down, you have a way to discipline yourself. Don't try to do three manuscripts a week. I wouldn't do more than one a week. You will do better on your other preparations if you have done one crisp manuscript a week. I think that brings a point of expectation to yourself and tends to carve your thoughts and preparation process in a way that otherwise isn't there.

Interviewer: Do you have any last thought for the preachers now reading your words—any comments or suggestions you would like to make?

Huffman: I would say this: Know your people, love your people, let them know you, and share yourself. I would encourage you to trust your people, to let them know your own pain and doubts and frustrations, yet with the positive understanding that God is at work in your life and we are growing together. Do not be afraid to speak about what you really believe. Trust the Holy Spirit more and just go for broke—be less worried about what people think, a little less concerned about criticism.

                                                    July/August 1990

PREACHING TO SEEKERS

Bill Hybels

Every weekend, some fifteen thousand persons make their way to the Chicago suburb of South Barrington, Illinois, to participate in the life of Willow Creek Community Church. Characterized by a contemporary worship style and a focus on appealing to unchurched persons, the church has been led for nearly two decades by Bill Hybels. Under his leadership, Willow Creek has developed a unique ministry that is now being studied and emulated by scores of churches around the United States.

Interviewer: Anyone who visits Willow Creek Community Church will quickly see that the overall worship style is very different—very nontraditional. What led you to adopt the kind of preaching style that you use at Willow Creek?

Hybels: What led us to the particular format we use was the realization that it's difficult to do evangelism and edification optimally in the same service. What we decided to do was to have a midweek edification worship service and devote our weekend services more toward outreach—Christianity 101 for seekers and new believers.

At Willow Creek we have two distinct preaching approaches. At our midweek service, we would most likely teach expositionally because that's a believers' service filled with people who already know Christ, love him, and simply want to be fed, challenged, and instructed from God's Word. At our weekend services, there are many skeptics, cynics, and investigators—people who are outside the family of God peeking over the fence to see what it's like inside. So our approach would tend to be more topical and more directed at some common ground—at the needs of unchurched people, showing the relevance of Scripture to the plight of mankind. One would tend to be more topical and the other more expositional.

Interviewer: Give me an idea, for example, of the kind of preaching you might be doing now in the weekend services versus what you're doing on Wednesday night.

Hybels: Well, I just finished a six-week series on spiritual gifts at the midweek service for our believers. I've done weekend series such as "Telling the Truth to Each Other," "Christianity's Toughest Competition," "Faith Has Its Reasons," "Fanning the Flames of Marriage," "Parenthood," and "Breaking the Chains That Bind You."

Interviewer: In the weekend services that are focused on the unchurched you take a more topical approach. How overt are you in your use of Scripture? Is there frequent use of Scripture, or is there simply an underlying scriptural basis for the more topical approach?

Hybels: I think the latter is a fair description, but it varies widely. For instance, on Father's Day this past year my sermon was entitled "Phantom Fathers"—how fathers fail and how their failure often breeds resentment in the lives of their children. I spoke right out of the story of David and Absalom. David failed as a father and created an enormous amount of resentment in the heart of Absalom, which created all kinds of complications later on. So I spoke from the narrative of the Old Testament on Father's Day; whereas, when I did a series about a year ago titled "The Age of Rage," I used the Ephesians passage, "Don't sin in your anger"—don't let the sun go down without trying to bring some form of resolution to it. In a series like that, I tend to use Scripture as the underlying authority for what I'm saying.

Interviewer: Have you found that your preaching style has changed based on where you are now as opposed to previous settings in which you were preaching?

Hybels: Actually, Willow Creek is my first senior pastorate, and it's the only church that I've preached in consistently for the last sixteen years, so I can't really answer that.

Interviewer: So your own preaching style has developed within this setting?

Hybels: Yes. The people have paid the price of me growing up in my preaching over the years and, quite frankly, they're still paying the price, I think!

Interviewer: How important do you think this particular approach to preaching is as a factor in Willow Creek being able to so effectively reach unchurched people?

Hybels: It's a major factor because unchurched people are not quick to relate to traditional preaching styles where the illustrations are about Moody and Spurgeon and missionaries. That's not the world they live in—those aren't the players that unchurched people relate to. As so many unchurched people told me before we started Willow Creek, "We dropped out of church. We don't go to church because they're giving answers to questions we're not even asking."

What we have attempted to do at Willow Creek with our weekend seeker services is to be very careful about addressing the whole counsel of God, but addressing it in as relevant a way as possible, because we want to get the ear of that unchurched person whose attention is not easy to capture and maintain.

Interviewer: During the '80s and into the '90s, we've had a lot of social change. The Chicago area, like most other parts of the country, has experienced a tumultuous period. Have you seen, even over the past eight or ten years, your preaching changing to adapt to some of those changes taking place?

Hybels: I'd say it's a very insightful question that you're asking. I have found a dramatic change in the sixteen years that Willow Creek has been in existence. In the mid to late '70s, if we led people to Christ through the preaching ministry of the church, the next challenge was to encourage people to shift over to the midweek service where they could receive expository teaching and get into small groups and become disciples.

Now in the '90s, we find that much of what we have to do is attempt to speak to people's brokenness, their addictions, their wounds, their victimizations. We're finding that instead of just discipling people we lead to Christ, we have to almost re-parent them before they're capable of being discipled because they have

> *Unchurched people are not quick to relate to traditional preaching styles where the illustrations are about Moody and Spurgeon and missionaries.*

lived with so much trauma. They have been wounded and broken so badly that most of the time some form of counseling is necessary. We regularly put on seminars sponsored by our counseling center on addictions and forms of violation and heartbreak that you really have to address if you're going to be relevant in today's world.

Interviewer: That's a different idea, the idea of healing as you reach people even before you can disciple them. How would you recommend a traditional pastor approach that whole idea in the preaching ministry?

Hybels: I think it's very tempting for traditional preaching styles to present Christ and the Word of God as the quick cure-all for whatever ailment is afflicting an individual today. I think that might be a little bit simplistic. If someone has been sexually molested, if someone grew up in the home of an alcoholic father, if someone has been beaten as a child, there are some deep psychological wounds that have to be carefully treated by trained

Christian counselors before those wounded people can thoroughly appropriate the promises and the precepts of Scripture.

Ideally, discipleship, preaching, and counseling should be integrated so all of that could work together in bringing a person toward fullness. We have found that if people are not being personally restored through Christian counseling or personal discipleship through a mentoring process, traditional preaching alone is probably not enough to restore many people to wholeness.

Interviewer: Tell me a little bit about your own approach to preaching—how you go about preparing a sermon, whether it be one for weekend or midweek. What approach do you take as you move through the preparation process?

Hybels: My approach would vary dramatically if I'm preaching to our midweek believers' service or our weekend service. For our midweek service, if we're preaching through a book of the Bible, I would take the rather conventional expository approach of reading the text, going through the correct hermeneutical steps to make sure I'm touching all the bases and doing the commentary work. Then I try to make that passage relate and live in the hearts of the people to whom I'm preaching.

I work very hard on application. I think the instructional part is the easier part of preaching; the points of application are exceedingly difficult to make relevant. I strive to keep it practical, to keep it applicable, to present Scripture in a way that believers walk away saying, "I know what the main emphasis was and I even have three or four ways I can put it into effect in my life tomorrow."

I find myself asking the famous two-word question all throughout my sermon preparation process, which is the phrase "So what?" Why is this important to the guy who just spent twelve hours in the loop of Chicago banging his head in the financial markets? He raced to the commuter train, his wife picked him up at the station, and he ate a sandwich in the car on the way out to the church. Why does he need to know what I'm saying? Of what importance is this to him? I work very hard on that so that people really drive away saying, "It was good to be in the house of the Lord and to sit under the Word, because I got something I could use in my life."

It's a little different from the weekend crowd because I can't take the conventional expository approach. If I say very strongly, "Thus saith the Lord," or, "Thus saith the Word of God," unchurched people say, "I don't buy your premise, so why should I listen to what you're saying?" So when I'm speaking to seekers, I tend to spend more time building bridges so that people see the logic in the instructions behind the Word of God.

I've done a series on the Ten Commandments a few times at our weekend services. When the Scriptures say, "Thou shalt have no other gods before me," you can preach that to a Christian audience and say, "Thus saith the Lord," and they'll do it—they

> *I find myself asking the famous two-word question all throughout my sermon preparation process, which is the phrase "So what?"*

accept that God rejects idolatry of any kind. In an unchurched crowd, the question is, "Why? Why is God hung up on exclusivity? What's the wisdom behind that commandment?" So I would spend time developing the idea that if you put your faith and trust in anything other than the true God of Scripture, it's going to disappoint you in your time of need. It's not going to touch your soul. It's not going to meet the longings in your heart. I would have to spend more time showing the wisdom behind the particular commandment.

Interviewer: Which service do you find to be easier to prepare?

Hybels: Oh, the midweek services by far!

Interviewer: The whole issue of application is one of the areas many pastors struggle with the most. Sometimes it's tempting to avoid it altogether because it's so tough. Are there particular approaches or tools, any elements that you have found to help you in developing good, authentic application?

Hybels: I think what helps in the application part of my preaching ministry is that I am in close relational contact with persons in my accountability group—couples that my wife, Lynne, and I fellowship with. I am very tuned in to what most men and women in our community are wrestling with.

When I'm giving a message in my "Parenthood" series, for instance, I keep in mind one of my closest friends who has three preschool children. He is at the end of his rope most of the time because of the frustration of knowing how to bring the proper balance between love and discipline. In preaching on that subject, I kept him and his family in mind during the whole preparation process so that others who would fall into that same category would benefit from the instruction and application I was making to him and his family.

Most of the time in my preaching, I'm really thinking of a few individuals who I know need instruction and application in the specific area that I'm talking about that day. In the "Age of Rage" series, there are some people in my immediate world who are being consumed with anger, and I knew that when I gave the practical steps—how to move from anger to resolve and do it authentically and biblically—I knew they'd be all ears. I had to do my homework carefully. I had to make sure my application was biblical, in general agreement with sound Christian psychological laws, and so forth.

Interviewer: Look ahead over the next several years as you see your church setting and the things that may be coming in the '90s. How do you see your preaching changing over the next several years?

Hybels: I see myself doing less of it.

Interviewer: Why is that?

Hybels: At Willow Creek we have transitioned to a team-teaching format. We have five services a week and we're just moving into six now. We have two midweek services, Wednesday night and Thursday night. Now this fall we're moving to two Saturday night and two Sunday morning services. I hit the wall a couple of years ago trying to do them all, so now we have a rotation where I quarterback a team of four teachers. I try to lead the rotation to play to the strengths of the teachers, yet keep the directional momentum to the preaching menu of the church.

I believe that more churches are going to move toward that as
pastors find out that they will tend to either preach well or lead
their church well; but if they're trying to do both, something's
going to suffer, and sometimes everybody suffers. So maybe we'll
be a prototype for the team-teaching approach.

The advantage to the congregation is they hear the voice of
God through different voice boxes. They discern the wisdom of
God through different personalities and gift mixes. The other
advantage is that the teachers get more preparation time, so that
what they bring to the congregation can be better researched,
more thoroughly prayed through, and applied to their own lives.
A lot of us pastors preach what we have not yet applied to our
own lives, because by the time we're trying to apply truth to ourselves, we're already in preparation for the next time up. That
often leads to some forms of hypocrisy—it's unintentional, but
it's almost inevitable.

I really believe that the church ought to be led by leaders and
taught by teachers—plural—and administrated by administrators, and so on. We're heading in that direction, and I think that's
exciting.

Interviewer: How often as the senior pastor do you find yourself preaching?

Hybels: Fifty percent of the time. Most churches only have
a Sunday morning service so that would mean twenty-six times.
In the course of the year, I'll probably speak twenty-six weekend
services, but also maybe eight or nine of our midweek services.
It's important to me to nourish and feed the core of the church
at our midweek services, and it's also important for me to be a
consistent communicator to the unchurched community in our
area.

Again, we make those decisions more by gift mix. Two of us
on the teaching team have very strong evangelism gifts with our
preaching, so we would tend to do more of the weekend services.
The other two tend to be a little stronger at the midweek services, so we would play to the strengths. One of the four of us is
a pure communicator who can really speak in either place effectively—that's not me, by the way!

Interviewer: When you do a weekend, you would take all four services?

Hybels: Correct, both Saturday night and both Sunday morning. That's the approach we're taking at this point. If we find out that that's too exhausting for one of the players, then we'll readjust and handle it differently.

Interviewer: How far ahead do you try to plan the preaching schedule for the church?

Hybels: We have it planned out for about nine months. We do that in community. It's very important for your readers to understand that the elders, the teaching team, a few staff members, and a few laypeople will huddle together and spend multiple retreats working out what we sense to be the direction of God on that matter. We spend a lot of time discerning the Spirit on the preaching menu.

Interviewer: When you do that planning, you're planning not only who's going to speak but also topics?

Hybels: We plan what the series is about, how many weeks, and which series should follow which to provide some sense of continuity. That's closely scrutinized by a group of very godly, discerning people, because if most pastors are honest, what they preached on in the last year will tend to reflect their own biases and strengths and so on. That's not necessarily what would serve the congregation best.

I think the best illustration of that is this: I was at one of the sermon planning sessions, and someone encouraged me to do a series on fear. I said, "Well, that's a good idea, do the rest of you have any other ideas?" I planned to pass on that idea, but one of the elders stopped me and said, "Bill, why don't you admit that you don't preach on fear because it's not a big problem for you because of the family you grew up in, the temperament you have, the personality you have, the faith you have. You don't wrestle much with fear." And I said, "Okay, that's true, I don't. Why don't you or one of the group here tell me if you do."

Then I listened for the next forty-five minutes, and it became very apparent to me that fear was an important subject in the lives of many people. So I wound up speaking on it for three weeks, and one of those messages became the most purchased tape of any sermon I did that year! So they were right, I was wrong, and the congregation would not have been served well, in part because of my blindness and the way I'm wired up.

Interviewer: How do you go about evaluating your preaching?

Hybels: I think probably the best way for a preacher to improve his preaching is to find some very discerning, godly people in the church who, by invitation of the teacher, will lovingly but truthfully evaluate each and every sermon in written form. They give a written evaluation shortly after the message is delivered for the purpose of stimulating that spiritual gift, challenging it to grow, developing it, and cheering it on.

I've done this for over ten years now, and all four teachers evaluate each other's messages. When I'm out of town and one of the other guys brings the message, I listen to it by tape and give a written evaluation of it. Again, the primary purpose of it is encouragement and cheering each other on as the Scripture implores us to do. We give constructive kinds of criticism that help us bump our preaching up a notch each time we do it. That's the thinking behind it.

I think the teachers at Willow Creek would say that the evaluation of their preaching has been what has pushed their gifts to higher levels, because that tends to be an area where the Christian community has taken a hands-off approach. When it comes right down to it, almost every other spiritual gift is evaluated by the congregation. If someone sings a solo and sings off pitch the whole time, they get the word that they'd better do something about improving their musical gifts or their gifts won't be in demand anymore. But a preacher can massacre a text, bore a congregation, and never touch a chord of interest in the life of a person in the church, and as he stands at the back door, the people file out and say, "Great job today." That kind of deception just continues ineffective preaching that eventually destroys the church.

We have decided that preaching should be affirmed or corrected—encouraged or rebuked—just like all the other gifts of the church. Preaching should be subjected to that with a loving, Christlike spirit by invitation of the pastor, with the kind of people he can trust and knows don't have hidden agendas. I could not take an evaluation from certain people in our church because they're grinding an ax, and it would be too painful for me. I'd feel too emotionally vulnerable. But there are other people who I know really love God and love me, but they love God more than they love me and they want to help me grow in my preaching. They want the church to receive the best kind of preaching it can receive from someone like me and the other teachers. That has been a tremendous help in improving our preaching.

Interviewer: In addition to your teaching team that evaluates one another, how many lay leaders would you say you pull into that group?

Hybels: About a half-dozen.

Interviewer: Do you give them a specific, written evaluation form?

Hybels: No, they usually do it on the front of the bulletin. I'm very clear with them, saying it helps me emotionally if they write the encouraging parts first. If they're going to make a criticism of some sort, I would appreciate it coming in the form of a recommendation. It's easy to say, "I didn't like point two." What I need to know is, "How would you have changed point two to make it better?"

I don't always follow each suggestion made. It's not just because someone makes a suggestion that I change something, but if four of six evaluators say that my illustration of the boy

> *We have decided that preaching should be affirmed or corrected, just like all the other gifts of the church.*

and the dog didn't work well, I'd better rethink the illustration of the boy and the dog to make sure that it's doing what I hoped it would do.

Many pastors are in multiple services. We make dramatic changes between the Saturday night and Sunday services. I remember recently one of our other teachers was really struggling with a message. He gave it Saturday evening, and if it's not sacrilegious to refer to it this way, I would have given him a C on Saturday night. We talked for an hour and a half after the service and made some changes on his message. At nine o'clock Sunday, it was about a B, and we worked for another thirty minutes after that. And when he gave it at eleven o'clock, it was right up there in the A- to A level. He learned throughout the whole process, so all of those are lessons that will serve him and our church well the next time out.

That's very important. Think about it—professional athletes have batting coaches, businessmen have consultants, government officers have advisors, so it only stands to reason that preachers need coaches. Preachers need people to get up next to them and say, "I think I saw something that could help you improve."

One of the evaluators whom I use regularly is an attorney, and he has impeccable logic. If I skip one step in the logical process, he's on me like a shirt. That's good for me because it challenges me when I'm putting the messages together. Another one of my evaluators is a theologian, so while the attorney watches my logic, the theologian watches my theology. Another one is a home-maker who is a "feeler" type. She will alert me to any off-the-cuff remarks I make that might be offensive or be considered insensitive by some members of the congregation. I have a wide variety of evaluators.

I even have one sort of nonchurch person. He's not a Christian yet, but he is a very wise, discerning man. I check with him and he gives me the reaction from someone outside the family of God. It sounds funny to have a nonchurch person evaluate your preaching. It's much less formal because he doesn't even come to church each week. But I'll call him on Monday, and I'll say, "Did that make sense to you? What could I improve? What didn't you get?" It's amazing what people get and what they don't get. So all of the feedback is very important.

January/February 1992

PREACHING
TO CHANGE LIVES

Richard Jackson

North Phoenix Baptist Church is one of the largest churches in America, with thousands of members, a national television ministry, and an international reputation for effective ministries and a powerful pulpit. Prior to his retirement, Richard Jackson stood behind that pulpit for over twenty years and led that church in its phenomenal growth and development.

Known widely for his effective biblical preaching, Jackson is a dynamic personality in and out of the pulpit.

Interviewer: You have established a reputation for effective biblical preaching. We are interested to know what biblical preaching means to you. How do you define the character of genuine biblical preaching?

Jackson: I don't think any other form of preaching is legitimate. God has promised, we remember, to bless his Word. He did not promise to bless by cleverness or eloquence. In fact, he did not promise to bless what I say *about* his Word, unless it is really based in the Word itself. I must interpret and apply his Word in the sermon, so I must speak about his Word, but I must do so faithfully. As I see it, biblical preaching brings Scripture alive in the "now" with application. All that is said about the text must grow out of the text and be faithful interpretation and application.

Interviewer: Where does the preacher begin this process? How does the intention and commitment to preach a biblical message find its beginning?

Jackson: I begin with the text. Now that is what you are supposed to say, but it really is the truth. I plan my preaching by working through the books of the Bible and preaching them through.

Lavonn Brown (pastor of First Baptist Church, Norman, Oklahoma) once said to me, "The only thing wrong with all the preaching we do is the preaching we do all the time." We must vary our form once in a while for the congregation's sake—and for our own!

I do very little thematic preaching, but some situations require it, so I go immediately to an appropriate text and find the message there, rather than bringing my thematic message to the text. We cannot bring the message to the text. I have no confidence in thematic preaching which finds the message in the theme; it must come from the text.

Interviewer: How do you find the message within the biblical text? How do you allow the text to speak within the sermon? This is the critical issue for most preachers seeking to be faithful to the task of biblical preaching.

Jackson: I have gone through a growth process on this point. I started out, like most young preachers, with a thematic approach. I went to seminary and learned something about homiletics and expository preaching, and in my early years, I took the text and dealt with what I determined to be its major theme—worked it out in points and the rest.

Then, a few years ago, I started a verse-by-verse exposition of the text. I had seen so much of this that was just a running homily by someone who read verses until he had something to say. I did not want to do that, so I started taking a verse-by-verse approach and combined that with the thematic method I had used earlier.

I found that I was preaching messages with too much content for one sermon, but God blessed his Word. I preached through Romans and the Gospel of John—not laborious messages, but I probably did more with each verse than I needed to do in the preaching context.

I have evolved now to the point where I take a larger text and am less detailed in the exposition. This varies from book to book. I preached through Matthew a few years ago and had one sermon for each chapter. I then went through Mark and John and found myself preaching about five sermons in each chapter. Now, as I am in Luke, I am preaching about two or three messages in each chapter. There are no hard-and-fast rules, but there is a natural balance.

Interviewer: How does this method work itself out in the context of the sermon? How do you find this natural balance in the text?

Jackson: Let me give you an example. Just a few weeks ago I preached on ministry as seen in Luke 7. There are four events recorded in that chapter—the healing of the centurion's son, the raising of the widow's son, John the Baptist's inquiry to Jesus, and the anointing of Jesus' feet. There are fifty verses in that chapter! But the four events were precisely what we needed to see as the ministry example of Jesus. I preached on Jesus as the Great Physician: "The Doctor Is In and He Will See You Now." We looked to Jesus as the model for ministry and found him ministering to the sick, the sorrowing, the searching, and the sinners.

I do not put a lot of emphasis on cute outline schemes. We can go overboard with alliteration, but it can be a very useful tool.

Interviewer: Fifty verses! Most preachers would blush at the idea of a fifty-verse text. Yet I see the natural balance in the simple exposition of this lengthy chapter.

Jackson: This is an extreme example! Fifty verses in any one sermon is a bit much, but it fit this situation. When the text is combined with a simple outline of application, it will remain in the congregation's mind. The people walked out of that service with those four forms of ministry firmly in mind. I hope they went home and read that chapter and learned more of it for themselves.

I don't believe in holding anything back for a later sermon. I may choose to leave something undeveloped, but not because I want to save it for a later sermon. I preach the great texts on

> ## *When the text is combined with a simple outline of application, it will remain in the congregation's mind.*

Wednesday night as well as Sunday morning. I think that if a preacher is really faithful, nothing will be held back for the next time. This was Charles Spurgeon's approach—he never held anything back. If God gave him an illustration or an application of a text, he did not hold it back in reserve for a later opportunity. It appears to me that we have to die with every sermon, as it were. We must pray that *this* sermon will be the best we have ever preached, or will ever preach.

Interviewer: You have been at North Phoenix Baptist Church for over twenty years. The task of preaching to one congregation for two decades presents a tremendous challenge. How has the task changed you and your preaching in those years?

Jackson: I have found myself growing in the delivery of the sermon. A seminary professor once said to me, "I'll bet you wish you could preach like I do." I said, "Yes!" He was a great preacher. Every gesture was perfect, every word fell gracefully from his lips. I was a crass young preacher. But that professor gave me a powerful word that day. He said, "It might surprise you to know that I have always longed to preach with the kind of force and power that you have." He went on to tell me that I should be true to myself and learn within my own natural and God-given style.

I have learned to tone down some of the physicality of my style. I am much more comfortable with silence than I was twenty years ago, and this impacts my preaching. I like to believe that I put a greater emphasis on the content of the text and less upon other matters. I know I have a better grasp of the text now than before.

Interviewer: Where do you see your preaching going in the future?

Jackson: This is far more exciting than the question of how I have changed in the past! I know that I have just now begun to learn, and entirely new opportunities are opening up for effective preaching right where I am serving. We must all evolve as preachers. I pray that I will be a much better preacher in the future than I have ever been.

Interviewer: Every preacher has found some key insights and practical discoveries which opened up new effectiveness in preaching. What practical suggestions would you offer other preachers?

Jackson: You know, I think I would answer this question differently than I would have just a few years ago. At the seminary, we are taught the necessity of textual application, but I don't think we really appreciate the importance of application when we are in seminary. This insight does not come from study—it comes from living with people. Application doesn't emerge from the ivory tower. We can come out of the study sounding like a commentary. The message must come alive as the preacher is in contact with real people.

On the other hand, the preacher who says, "I will just be with my people," and does not study cannot really preach a biblical sermon. This preacher may be very popular, but there will not be much substance.

The practical course is to spend time in the Word and in study—and then have all this in mind when you are with people. These must be people from all walks of life—not just church members. I may spend time with someone on the golf course. Their comments, their questions, their concerns—all these work in me and work themselves out in my message.

We must be something between the "walking commentary" and the "jolly good preacher" who neglects study in favor of personal contact. We must have a pastor's heart and a firm calling, matched with a great love for people. We must then saturate our minds with the text of Scripture and come to the moment of delivery ready and equipped for the Holy Spirit to do something creative and mysterious.

I am absolutely awed by what happens in the moment of delivery. When the preacher is fully in the Word and in the worldly situation something incredible will happen.

Interviewer: Your excitement and confidence is tangible. This must be a critical ingredient of the mix which produces a Richard Jackson—and a North Phoenix Baptist Church.

Jackson: I believe that the secret to great preaching is the preacher's willingness to die in the preaching experience. I don't know any other way to do it but to hang it out, to be transparent and open. A fellow said to me last night, "Thank you for being real." Now that can be a cliché, but I think I know what he meant. I did not preach a sermon last night which would impress the classical homileticians. We can all do that. We all know some "cutesy" techniques and we are all tempted to use them. Yet the folks who flew me across the country to preach that message were not looking for someone to demonstrate technical skills; they were looking for a message that would make a difference in their human lives.

I have understood this much since I preached my first sermon at age fifteen—that I was to make a difference in someone's life. If we do not walk into the pulpit with that purpose, the message will not go anywhere or speak to anyone.

Interviewer: North Phoenix Baptist Church has grown to be one of the largest churches in the United States. The pulpit of that great church has a well-deserved reputation for evangelistic preaching. How do you define or describe biblical preaching?

Jackson: This issue is the same—a basic concern for people and a realization that preaching is to change lives. Evangelism, however, is an atmosphere God creates, not something a preacher brings about by clever preaching.

I mentioned the sermon I recently preached from Luke 7. I spent thirty minutes of that sermon speaking directly to Christians—they were the focus of that message. Yet for the last five or six minutes I spoke of the woman who anointed Jesus' feet and identified her as a sinner reached by God's grace. Jesus ministers to those who sin, and then they recognize their sin and can be forgiven. I made this application, and said that the church must minister to those in sin because of our Savior's example. I just extended the application of the text to the invitation for sinners to come to faith and salvation. I just gave the invitation. You know, we had some twenty professions of faith.

Many people have the idea that a preacher who has that kind of response, who baptizes large numbers of people each year, must get up and holler, "Jesus saves!" for thirty minutes and give a twenty-minute pressure invitation. I preach for thirty to thirty-five minutes and 90 percent of the message is almost always addressed to believers.

You know, the evangelistic application is *always* there. I don't have to create it. The evangelistic message is shot through the Bible—it is God's heart. If we get up and give a method appeal or a high-pressure appeal, we make God look like a beggar. If we just preach the Word, extend a dignified appeal, and provide an opportunity for response, it will happen. That is evangelistic preaching—and that is Christian preaching.

July/August 1989

THE POWER
OF EXPOSITION

R. T. Kendall

Few churches in the world enjoy the international reputation Westminster Chapel has established for excellence in biblical preaching. Located just a few meters from Buckingham Palace, Westminster Chapel has been a powerful fixture on the religious scene for several generations. Lions of the pulpit such as G. Campbell Morgan and Martyn Lloyd-Jones thundered across England and throughout the world from the stately pulpit of Westminster Chapel.

The current steward of that pulpit is R. T. Kendall, an American minister. Educated at the University of Louisville and Southern Baptist Theological Seminary in the United States, and with a doctor of philosophy degree from Oxford University, Kendall brings a rich background to his ministry at Westminster Chapel. He is the author of several books, including *Jonah, God Meant It for Good, Stand Up and Be Counted,* and *Once Saved, Always Saved.*

Interviewer: From the vantage point of an American currently preaching in one of the most famous churches in Great

90

Britain, how do you evaluate the current state of preaching in the world?

Kendall: My first thought is that preaching is not given much prominence. The emphasis these days seems to be on worship rather than preaching. Preaching is almost perfunctory in some churches rather than the central act of expectation within worship.

Interviewer: What do you see as the difference between the condition of preaching in England and the place of preaching in American churches?

Kendall: In England, even more so than in America, preaching has had a preeminent place in the church; that is less true now. This is explained partly by the incredible increase in secularism among the British, a general decline of interest in religion. It may also be explained by a lack of great preachers.

Interviewer: How would you describe your philosophy and theology of preaching?

Kendall: I think the preaching of the Word should be the center of the worship event. The centrality of preaching is what God will honor—assuming, of course, that this preaching is the faithful preaching of the gospel and truth.

We must acknowledge that 1 Corinthians refers to the foolishness of what is preached as well as the human instrument of preaching. But I think that preaching—and even the traditional

> *I believe that God will honor a church that is making preaching central—and a preacher who is making exposition the center of his preaching.*

role of the preacher in the pulpit—should be given prominence. It has not always been so, and it should not be done at the expense of other forms of witness and ministry. Personal witness is good preaching, and faithful preaching can also come through a hymn, but I think a symptom of the superficiality of the church and the declining interest in the church on the part of some sectors of society is the decline of preaching.

I admit also that if preachers are not very committed, the preaching will not be powerful, and there will be, of course, little interest. I believe that God will honor a church that is making preaching central—and a preacher who is making exposition the center of his preaching. This is crucial. Preaching must be expository.

Interviewer: As I understand the preaching heritage of Westminster Chapel, G. Campbell Morgan called himself an exegetical preacher, and there was a dramatic shift in that tradition when Martyn Lloyd-Jones succeeded him and began a ministry of what he defined as expository preaching. You describe your own preaching as expository. How do you define this kind of preaching?

Kendall: Expository preaching is simply making clear the meaning of the text and showing its relevance and application for the lives we live. Though Morgan and Lloyd-Jones used different terms to describe their preaching styles, both were really expository in method. Lloyd-Jones was perhaps more theologically minded than Morgan, and Morgan was perhaps more biblical than theological in the pulpit, but both were very effective expositors of the Word.

Interviewer: Before your call to Westminster Chapel as pastor, you had begun a series on the prophet Jonah as a visiting minister. Before that series was complete, you were to accept a call to Westminster Chapel as minister. How did that come about?

Kendall: That is a most remarkable story. When I came to Westminster Chapel, it was to be for six months as a visiting minister. I had no intention of staying beyond that. As I thought and prayed about what to preach, my thoughts came to rest on Jonah. I had never preached on Jonah before, but I thought in terms of eight sermons for eight Sundays on Jonah.

Yet when I worked on the very first sermon, I had an experience like nothing I had ever had before. The thoughts just kept pouring into my mind. When I stepped into the pulpit for that first sermon, I did not get beyond the very first verse of the book.

As it happened, my plan for eight sermons expanded week by week into twenty-three. After the sixth sermon, I happened to have lunch with John R. W. Stott. He chuckled and was amazed that anyone would preach in Jonah for six weeks. Neither of us knew that it would expand to twenty-three!

Interviewer: In most American evangelical churches, it would be considered unusual for any series of expository sermons to last through twenty-three messages, much less a series based on the prophet Jonah. Nevertheless, this tradition of long expository series seems to be well established at Westminster Chapel. How does your method of expository preaching lend itself to series of this duration?

Kendall: I almost never announce in advance how long a series will be. Just now, however, I am engaged in an experiment to see if I can discipline myself to keep within twelve sermons on the twelve verses of Isaiah 53. I knew if I did not announce the length of this series, I would never get out of that great chapter of Isaiah. I have forced myself to push on in this case, and the series is coming along. Nevertheless, I would not want to make this my usual practice. I recently completed a series on 1 John of over one hundred sermons.

Interviewer: Westminster Chapel is an inner-city congregation. How does this context inform and shape your preaching?

Kendall: I do not think that the context determines what I preach or how I present the message. It is the case, however, that we are attempting to reach our immediate area in a way not always attempted in the past.

I believe God honors preaching as a means of reaching those around us at Westminster Chapel. We are better known two thousand miles away from us than we are in our own neighborhood. Visitors come regularly from around the world, but not much from the immediate area. Nevertheless, for the last few years we have sought to reach our immediate area and have reached hundreds.

Westminster Chapel has never been a traditional local church, a neighborhood church. Lloyd-Jones said to me that Morgan had said to him that Westminster Chapel was not a church, but a center for preaching. My vision is to be both.

Interviewer: You have inaugurated the practice at Westminster Chapel of inviting persons to make a public pledge of their faith. Many American churches end every service with such an invitation. How is this done at Westminster Chapel?

Kendall: With the public pledge, a person confesses publicly what has taken place in the heart. This to me was more biblical than inviting persons forward to receive salvation. They come to confess their salvation rather than to receive it. Some come who do not really know what they are doing, and we have counselors there to talk to them. There is, we feel, a theological integrity to this—and a biblical mandate.

Interviewer: What are your hopes for preaching? What would you like to see happen in the pulpits of the world?

Kendall: I pray that preachers would be mastered by the text, that they would learn the art of bowing before the text with such a high view of Scripture that they hear the very Word of God. When one hears this voice, the text is necessarily taken more seriously, and the preacher is less likely to impose his own meaning on the text.

The greatest weakness of preachers on both sides of the Atlantic is the tendency to come to the text with a preconceived notion of what the text means, and then to hijack the text with no feelings of guilt whatsoever. The preacher can easily have no clue what Paul really meant, or Jesus really said, but come to a text to make it mean what *they* want to say.

September/October 1988

THE WITNESS
OF PREACHING

*Thomas G. Long
and John Killinger*

Two of the most insightful minds in the world of homiletics are Thomas G. Long, Patton Professor of Preaching and Worship at Princeton Theological Seminary, and John Killinger, Distinguished Professor of Theology and Culture at Samford University in Birmingham, Alabama.

Interviewer: Tom, your book, *The Witness of Preaching,* provides some real insight into the nature of the preaching task. Tell us a little about the purpose of that book.

Long: Well, what I was trying to do in that was to create a basic textbook in which every phase of the preaching task would be touched, and all of it would grow out of a coherent vision and theory of the theology of preaching. The place I thought to begin in terms of developing a coherent understanding of preaching was with the image of the preacher.

I looked over the homiletical literature of the last fifty to seventy-five years, and it's been amazing to see how much homiletical thought has been generated out of basic figures of speech around the function of the preacher. And I identified three of those that have been in the literature.

I talked about the preacher as *herald,* which is really out of the Barthian movement. And I talked about the preacher as *pastor,* which has come, really, out of the Harry Emerson Fosdick model of preaching—life-situation preaching, the therapeutic preaching model. And then, more recently, the preacher as *storyteller.*

I found all three of those images to be extremely important and valuable, but limited in various ways. I suggested that the New Testament image of the preacher as *witness* was one that was superior to those others, and could afford a way of understanding the task of preaching that could pull together what we do with the Scripture, what we do with the structure, how the listener is involved, the role of the church in preaching—all of that falls into place once you put the image of witness into the foreground.

So I tried, then, to execute that image throughout the book in terms of all the aspects of the craft of putting a sermon together and delivering it.

Interviewer: In *The Witness of Preaching,* how do you separate that from simply the idea of preacher as evangelist? For someone just hearing the title, it would be easy to assume that you're discussing preaching as it relates to communicating the gospel in evangelism. How do you differentiate between those two images?

Long: At one level, I wouldn't differentiate between them. A preacher as evangelist in the broadest term is one who speaks the "evangel," who speaks the Good News. But generally speaking, it's been used in a smaller sense to mean one who takes the gospel out to the world that has not heard it and does the kind of public, missionary sort of preaching.

Preacher as witness is really a courtroom image. In the courtroom terminology, a witness appears in a trial in which the truth is the matter at stake. And the witness is not different from the ordinary round of citizen, except that the witness has seen and heard something, and then swears—is set apart, is ordained—to tell the truth, the whole truth, and nothing but the truth about it.

I think that's a good image for preaching. Moltmann says that the one who preaches comes from the community, then walks and turns and speaks and acts in the name of Christ. So the witness actually comes from the community—it's the community at large, the church, that has the interest in the truth at heart. And it sets apart one of its citizens, one of its persons, to take on the task of witnessing. So that person then goes to Scripture seeking to hear and see something, to encounter the voice of the text. That person carries with her or with him all of the questions and concerns and needs of the community from which he or she comes, but goes to Scripture prepared to hear whatever Scripture wishes to say about that need or action. Then the person turns and tells the truth about what has been seen and heard.

Sometimes the truth that is told answers or responds to those questions that the community has. Sometimes, as Barth says, it calls them into question, but the witness is always prepared to testify to what is true. It is no accident, then, that the word in the New Testament for witness is *martyr,* because sometimes bearing witness to the truth carries with it a great price.

Killinger: I've read Tom's book, and it's excellent. I think it is a very meaningful characterization of preaching, partly because what we're dealing with is mystery. I like to think of the image as being enlarged somewhat to be that of a mystery story in which not just one witness but many witnesses are taken into account. I think for me, at a personal level, preaching has been far more than simply witnessing to a tradition; it's been trying to listen to all the witnesses in many places and to be able, as I listen to those witnesses, to know, as you suggest, the truth of the mystery.

And yet there's always an elusive character to that truth for me. I feel like a maverick in lots of ways—that I, to this point in my life, have never been totally satisfied with any witness I've heard. I hear this witness, and I hear that witness, and the truth keeps shifting a little bit. I expect the business of listening to witnesses and then making whatever witness I have to make will be a lifelong project.

Long: I think that's very helpful. The task of witnessing is a very local activity. That is to say, it occurs in *this* place, with *this* person speaking to *these* people about what has been said, heard, and experienced, as they seek *their* mission in *this* time and place.

That's why I think it is rather remarkable that we have moved, in our own time, away from the nationally recognized pulpit figures. I mean, if you were on a committee thirty years ago trying to find a baccalaureate preacher at a school, you could come up with a lot of names, and then see if you could get one. Today

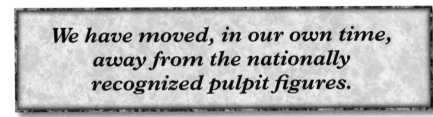

We have moved, in our own time, away from the nationally recognized pulpit figures.

such committees have a tough time coming up with names, and I think that's because our understanding of what makes for excellent preaching has moved much more into a local setting. It doesn't travel as well, it doesn't publish as well, perhaps. We're struggling with the mission at this place, and one bears witness in this courtroom to the concern for the truth that is a very local sort of event, which means that a single witness can't claim to encompass it all. We have a cloud of witnesses.

Killinger: One reason for their difficulty in finding names might be that Christendom has disintegrated in our time, and that the laypeople who are out looking don't know what they're looking for. I'm afraid that we don't have the sense of solidarity in Christendom that we've had. Now that's the flip side of what you're saying . . .

Long: No, I would agree with that. I think it is true that the Constantinian synthesis of Christendom has dissolved. The *New York Times* is no longer interested in publishing summaries of the great preachers in the pulpits on Sunday.

Interviewer: Do you think television has affected that also? The preaching they watch on Sunday morning on television, or on cable, or wherever they're watching, is by nature a very different kind of preaching than what, in past years, characterized the great preachers.

Long: I have some hunches that the television preachers that sort of parade across the whole landscape probably have less effect than some of us fear. I don't think they do very good preaching. I think it's superficial. I think it massages the *zeitgeist* of the culture. I don't run into a lot of laypeople who really look to those preachers as the exponents of the Christian faith, so I'm wondering about the size of their audience and the real impact in our culture. They're an interesting phenomenon.

I'm much more concerned about their local imitators; that is to say, people who do the same sort of baptizing of the cultural ethos in a local setting. I think they're far more dangerous because that ethos shows up when pastoral care is given. Because they are the pastors, they've had the reinforcement of preaching, whether their message itself is faithful or not. So I guess I'm not too worried about the television preachers, but I am worried about their imitators in a local setting.

Killinger: You don't think they're really witnesses, in other words.

Long: I don't.

Killinger: They haven't seen anything. They don't have anything, really, to tell.

Long: That's right.

Killinger: But they're manufacturing something out of consumer materials which they know that people will want to hear instead of really talking about it.

Long: I couldn't agree more. The collapse of Christendom and the breakup of the understanding of the nature of the gospel in the church, I think, point to a shift that we're going to experience in preaching, and I'd be very interested to know what John thinks about this.

The oldest textbook we've got about preaching that we know anything about is Augustine's *De Doctrina Christiana: Book IV.* In there, he borrows a line from Cicero to describe the purposes of preaching. He says, "The purposes of preaching are to teach, to delight, and to persuade," by which he means a very specific thing. And I think that's right, in a way.

I do think that also describes phases in the history of preaching. Sometimes we have been in a teaching mode—I think the Reformation was a bursting forth of the teaching mode of preaching. I think we've sometimes been in the ethical mode. You can see that in the Rauschenbusch movement. And I think for the past fifteen or twenty years, we've been in the delight mode in preaching. The whole emphasis on narrative and story has been a way of reinvigorating the pulpit with its ability to inflame the imagination. It's been good. We've learned a lot. I think we have discovered, however, the task of teaching has been neglected in the pulpit, and we've got congregations that no longer know the biblical materials, no longer have the theological vocabulary in their repertoire. Without losing what we've learned in the narrative phase, I think we're going to return much more to the task of teaching in the pulpit.

Killinger: How do you think that will happen, Tom, with an eighteen-minute homily? I mean, what can you possibly teach in the present liturgical setting? Are we talking about something that's much bigger, that is, the Sunday school, the Wednesday night meeting, other opportunities for people to . . .

Long: Yes, I don't think it's going to be restricted to the pulpit, because we can't do the whole task there. But I think the keynote is set there in terms of teaching. I'm attracted to Ellis Nelson's book *How Faith Matures,* in which he points out the difficulties that many parishes are having with Sunday school as the primary way of doing education in the life of the church. He really says that what we need to do is—well, he's not negative about the Sunday school as an institution, but he thinks we really need to back up and think of the totality of the congregational life as the educational ethos. What a congregation does—how they behave together as a group—is the educational environment.

I can testify to that. The Christian education that I really got, that was deep, occurred not so much in the Sunday school classroom as participating in the common round of congregational life as a child. And if the task of the pulpit can be to lift those moments up and interpret them—what does it mean that we behave this way and do these things in this place?—then that becomes the educational moment that is not cut off in congregational life, but is very much attached to it.

I also think that even in an eighteen-minute sermon we can take a vocabulary word like *grace* and begin to give that back to people. I think we can at least begin. The Black church has never forsaken the task of telling the biblical story in such a way that the congregation owns it, knows it, lives it, and has it as a part of their repertoire. I think we're going to see some more of that. The fact that the sermons are short, though, is a disadvantage in the teaching.

Killinger: You know, one word that I thought of when you were talking about Augustine is the word *discover.* Teaching, inclining the will, and delighting are all involved in the single task of discovering something, which is related to witness of something. That the sermon, even a brief sermon, is able to put us on the road to discovery—that may be the key to successful television evangelists, as well as to what the local pastor does in the pulpit. There is enough time there to pique the interest, to put a clue in front of somebody as to what truth is about, to show where people can move, how they can look, where they can turn to find something for their lives.

I think part of what has been wrong with our approach to Christianity—not just the pulpit, but the whole community—for the last thirty, forty, fifty years has been that we have tried to prepackage things and give them to people instead of involving

> *The sermon, even a brief sermon, is able to put us on the road to discovery.*

them in the search. And that leaves us in a nation where we have experienced the "dumbing-down" of everything—the dumbing-down of education, the dumbing-down of the church, the dumbing-down of the interplay between government and people, almost everything you can think of. It leaves us in a very precarious situation if we're no longer piquing people's interest to learn for themselves, to be individuals in search of something.

You know, I quite agree with what Ellis Nelson says, that there's something about being in the community that makes us teachable. We learn, we imbibe, we absorb by osmosis from the community, but if the community doesn't have anything beyond just the fact of getting together and repeating clichés, dwelling in a land of effete images and so forth, then something's got to be done to raise the level of the community.

So I come back to the word *discover.* I think we've got to discover something, and maybe, just maybe, at this point in our history, the thing that's going to save us is the witness, not of our own traditions in this country, but of the new traditions emerging in Africa, Asia, and other places. So for me witnessing means that we've got to do an awful lot of listening to the emerging witnesses in other places.

Long: And that makes the breakdown of Christendom not altogether bad news.

Killinger: It's been very personal to me, I think, being in Los Angeles for three years and trying to minister in a run-down church in the center of a place that has become multiethnic and everything else. I felt the impact of the world coming in on that and the breaking down of the old structures. It was very, very dynamic to me. I have this sense that we've got to discover something good out of the collapse of Christendom.

Just as the Reformation occurred out of the collapse of the Christendom of the Middle Ages, I think we're on the verge of breakthroughs, but American Christianity, by and large, is not aware of it yet. I think some really dynamic leaders are going to emerge in the next twenty, thirty, forty years and show us the way. Their witness is going to be very important, but I think we need to listen more sensitively to other places than we have been in order to hear the shape that witness is going to take.

Long: I agree. The level of awareness in the American church about the erosion of our consensus with the culture . . . I suspect that you're right, that our level of awareness is not very high, although I do think that varies from region to region. I think it is becoming very clear to churches in the Northeast, for example, that they no longer are in a position of dominance in the culture. It's probably less so in the Southeast—where my roots are—there is still much more of a handshaking with the dominant culture. But I think it's a matter of time, and it will become apparent to all of us.

Killinger: It's an exciting time in which to be a witness, but it's also a very precarious time. It bears out what you said about the danger of being a witness, the martyr aspect of it, that you can easily get clobbered by your own community today because you're not satisfied with cliché witness. Because you're searching for that edge of a word, a cutting word, that is just being formed in the midst of a new world community.

Interviewer: How does the preacher deal with that? In your preparation and when you stand in the pulpit, how do you come to grips with that change, and do the kind of teaching, Tom, that you talk about, that's becoming increasingly necessary? How do you suggest the pastor respond to that kind of challenge?

Long: To the challenge of the multiple voices in the world, and . . .

Interviewer: And the fact that his or her own congregation may be increasingly less aware of their own tradition, much less the other traditions that they're hearing.

Long: Well, I think that we do, and we've already started to do, a different kind of exegesis of the text for preaching. More and more of the recently trained ministers are very much aware of the fact that a text can be manhandled by critical approach. Every critical approach narrows your range of possibilities besides giving you some depth. The historical critical method which has been reigning supreme—which I am a believer in, I think we ought to take a good healthy dose of it every day—is nonetheless also limited in its capacity to see the range of possibilities in the text. I mean the Lone Ranger style of exegesis, where it's just you and the Bible, with your little range of methods.

Now we're aware of the fact that you need to have a seminar. You need to construct—in your mind, at least—a seminar around the text, in which multiple voices are brought in, as a way of seeing the multiple possibilities that are there in a text. If you're American, that means voices from the Third World; if you're a male, that means a woman's understanding of the text; if you're an adult, a child's perspective on the text; if you are White, a Black or oppressed minority's understanding of the text.

Killinger: I think there's also another dimension to that, that not only do we need to keep all of those aspects of the text in mind, but we also need somehow to maintain a kind of ambivalence toward textual preaching itself—to realize that the minute we choose the text, that we have narrowed the witness. In a sense, that the witness is even "transtextual," that it comes from many voices outside the biblical tradition as well.

Long: The question of a congregation's awareness of its tradition, and the value of a particular tradition, is a controversial question. And I suppose you could run in two separate directions with that question if you were a person of goodwill and understood that the gospel transcends a particular heritage.

One would be that a tradition is an embarrassment in a way, that it is a dividing marker between you and the global Christian community. I think that's true, but that's not the direction I want to run. I think, as a matter of fact, that as you get more ecumenical, and more able to speak in partnership with other Christians, the more aware you are of your own tradition, your own

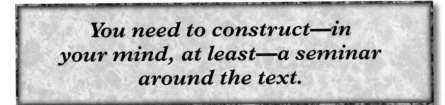

You need to construct—in your mind, at least—a seminar around the text.

heritage. That fact is that none of us speaks as a kind of universal Christian; we're always speaking out of a particular place and location. So the more we're in touch with the place and location in which we stand, the better we're able, then, to communicate with others.

I think of it as a neighborhood of houses. The Joneses live here, and the Kims live here, and the Smiths live there, and the Longs live there. And the more they are aware of their own stories, their own genealogies, their own backgrounds, and their own convictions and values, the better neighbors they can be, the more access they can have to their neighbors. I think the Christian faith is like that too.

So as a Presbyterian—I am a preacher in a Presbyterian church—I want that congregation to understand the Reformed tradition is an attempt to speak toward the totality of the Christian witness. It is a particular accent, a family accent, that I want them to learn and enjoy, and also become aware that it's not the whole, it's not the totality of the Christian faith.

Killinger: That's a good image. But the problem for the minister, always, is how do you enhance that sense of the family tradition without making people think that's all there is? You have to make people aware of the sacredness of other traditions as well, and be able to go down to somebody else's house and understand another tradition.

Interviewer: If we could, let's go back and touch on a topic that was raised earlier. So many books and articles are saying to the pastor, "When you preach, you've got to use narrative, you can't use the old 'three-points-and-a-poem' style that you learned in seminary. You've got to change and emphasize story." Tom talked about that as being a very healthy movement that has taken place, but at the same time, it's cost us in terms of the teaching ministry of the pulpit. Is it possible to merge those two elements of story and teaching? We discussed using narrative in the pulpit and then teaching in other settings. Is it possible to merge those two in some way in the pulpit itself?

Long: One of the reasons I like the witness image is because the witness is not restricted to a single mode of communication. Sometimes the witness is asked to tell the story: "Just tell your story." Sometimes the witness is asked to listen to facts: "Just listen to facts." That is to say, the nature of the thing being pointed to governs the structure of the communication required to do it, as well as the capacities of those who hear.

One of the flaws of the storytelling movement has been to privilege the narrative genre in Scripture and otherwise. It seems to me that what we've got in the Bible is a collection of genres, each of which was called forth because the richness of the gospel cannot be spoken in a single voice. Narrative voice is very important, but it's not the only voice.

Sometimes the community gets to the place that it needs ethical instruction. Sometimes the community says, "Yes, but how *was* Jesus Lord?" In that case, systematic reflection of some kind is needed. Sometimes it simply wants to cry in lament form, the poetic lament form, or give thanks in the doxological form.

All of these are voices that the Christian faith assumes under particular circumstances, and I think it's incumbent upon the pulpit not to restrict this chorus down to a single solo narrative voice. I think our key into that is to pay attention to the rhetorical strategies, as it were, of the Scripture itself when we preach— to recognize that the epistolary form, proverbial form, or parabolic form are not simply arbitrarily chosen vessels. These forms govern some of the power of the text itself and the meaning of the text itself. The literary rhetorical form in which the text comes is instructive to the preacher. It gives us freedom to assume a range of styles, structures.

The "three-points-and-a-poem" style has been much maligned, and if it is the only style used, it communicates, over time, that the Christian faith is a set of propositions. But avoid it altogether and we lose the capacity that it brings to teach clearly.

Killinger: From a historical perspective in the teaching of homiletics, it seems to me that the experimental period we went through in the '60s and '70s, which we're still deriving benefits from, was a lot like what happened in the theater of the absurd with Samuel Beckett and other playwrights like him. It was not the kind of theater that was going to last very long. It was experimental in nature; it destroyed the old classical Shakespearean, Ibsenian kind of theater and permitted something new to be born in our time.

And if you go to the theater now, whether it's David Mamet, Harold Pinter, or Tom Stockard, you get the new freedom that has come from those extreme experimentalists who were tearing up the nature of theater, who were following the idea that you turn the lights on to the audience and create havoc in the theater so that people are disoriented. Instead of putting on a well-made play, you assault the consciousness of the audience.

That couldn't last, but it did bequeath something to the modern writers of theater, who give us story in the continuous form, more or less, as we once had it, but with a freshness, with a new freedom to experiment in little ways and to make us see things better in theater.

And I think today preaching is enjoying, as you suggest, Tom, this sense of freedom to experiment with form in order to get the message across, or sometimes not just to *preach* a message, but to *be* message. The freedom of the medium becomes a message in itself, a way to say something about the nature of Christianity.

Interviewer: You referred a minute ago to some of the great preachers. One of the questions I am frequently asked is, "Who are the best preachers in America?" Who are two or three of the pulpit voices that you two particularly enjoy right now?

Long: I work every year with Fred Craddock, who I think—both in terms of his own preaching style and the way he thinks about preaching—has made a dramatic impact, not only on me, but on a lot of people. I also like Barbara Lundblad, a Lutheran from New York City. She is on *The Protestant Hour* as one of the Lutheran preachers, along with a colleague named John Vanorsdall, who has also been influential to me. Barbara's sermons are

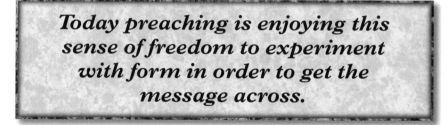

Today preaching is enjoying this sense of freedom to experiment with form in order to get the message across.

very sturdy, very clear. John's are poetic and evocative of mystery. I like Jim Forbes at Riverside Church. I find him to be stimulating, exciting. He brings the passion to the pulpit that many of us lack, and I find myself energized by him.

Killinger: I'm very fond of our friend and colleague here in Birmingham, John Claypool, at St. Luke's Episcopal Church. I'm always mystified a little bit by what it is I like about somebody. In John's case, I think a lot of it has been the continuing struggle that I've felt in him. Back to the old witness terminology, but John's been trying to identify what the truth is in his tradition, and at the same time, to identify what is untruth in his tradition, so he can move beyond that.

Long: You feel the struggle.

Killinger: Yes. I have a sense of the meaning of the struggle itself. The last time I heard John was during Lent, and he preached a sermon that—if I were being critical in terms of how it struck the audience—I would say was too personal, too much of his own psychological struggle at the moment. I'm not sure how many people were really participating at the level at which he was talking about it. But it was a witness to me that he was struggling, and that he was willing to talk about it. I like that very much.

Another person that I don't hear talked about very much—I think because he's way down in San Diego and who in the world knows what's going on in San Diego—is Mark Trotter. Mark is at First Methodist Church there, and he puts a lot into his preaching, works very hard on it. And yet his preaching comes across as a kind of smooth dialogue with what's happening in the daily lives of his people. He always has a keen theological insight, but there is a casualness, an *apparent* casualness, about the approach that is very winning to me. I admire the kind of offhanded style he achieves in talking to people in a culture like that around San Diego, with people who are not terribly church-conscious about the mysteries of the faith and of life.

January/February 1991

PREACHING
THE EMPTY TOMB

Max Lucado

Max Lucado has become known in recent years through a series of widely read books. That writing ministry grows out of his preaching as pastor of the Oak Hills Church of Christ in suburban San Antonio, Texas. The growing church currently runs about twelve hundred on Sunday morning.

Interviewer: The Lenten and Easter season is obviously one of the most important times for preaching as our minds are focused on the gospel. How do you go about preparing for preaching in that season? What are some of the special concerns you bring to preaching around the Easter season?

Lucado: My primary concern is that during the Easter season, people who have not been at church often all year long suddenly appear. Primarily on Easter Sunday and even a little before, and hopefully a lot afterwards, you'll have a good surfacing of fringe members or nonmembers. The burden that I feel during this time is to clearly articulate the promise of the empty tomb and the crucified Savior. That's my task during that month. I feel if I were to let April or March, wherever Easter falls that given year, pass without articulating three or four times that month why Jesus died and the implications of the empty tomb, then I would have missed a chance to be a billionaire. I would have missed an extraordinary opportunity.

I believe that just the nature of the changing seasons opens people up. They've been enclosed, they've been caved in all winter long and now spring is starting to open up, the promise of summertime is there. Then you have an opportunity to tell them about the death, burial, and resurrection of Jesus Christ. It's just an incredible opportunity.

I try, when I do that, to keep in mind that there are three solutions that the cross brings to human existence. I call them the three Fs on the human report card—failure, futility, and finality. That makes a great sermon outline. The first Easter I preached in the church, that was my sermon outline. Since then, I've gone back and I've changed it every year, but basically it is the same thing. The cross deals with failure, my mistakes; the cross deals with futility, my reason to be here; and the cross deals with finality, my grave. Unless I can deal successfully with those three elements of life, I haven't lived.

I remember when we were missionaries in Brazil—we went to Brazil to start this church, and we thought that immediately people were going to flock to hear us. I'll never forget the first few Sundays when we had no one there. We'd rented a storefront and some small rooms. We could barely speak Portuguese. I don't know why we didn't think of this, but if I were a Brazilian, I wouldn't have attended either.

Many Brazilians are involved in spiritism—it's an intellectual voodoo religion—and so their comment to us would be, "Why would we come into a small storefront to hear a bunch of Gringos speak sloppy Portuguese when we can go into this beautiful cathedral, hear this wonderful music, have the professor (what they often called the spirits) guide us into speaking with the dead, see them offer sacrifices for the dead (they'd offer chickens), or go through the ceremonies that are very emotional and intriguing—everyone dressed in white? It is an incredible event to attend, with thousands of people there. Why should we come over there and hear you guys when we can go to one of these arenas?" That really shook my theological tree down to its basic roots and I walked away with the question: What do we have to offer?

Easter tells us what we have to offer. We offer an answer for finality, for futility, and for failure. That's what I try to do, look into those three areas. The people who are there just that one Sunday, Lord willing, will come back because you're answering the questions they have.

Interviewer: Isn't that really the question that every pastor now faces in any community in America? People say, "Why should I come listen to you with all the things I have to do around here?"

Lucado: Exactly. I really think that the questions people are asking are so different now than they were when I was growing up. When I was growing up the question people asked was "Which church?" Today the question people are asking is "Why church? Why go to church at all?" No longer can we afford the luxury of thinking that the people who are sitting in our pews are going to be there every Sunday. We have to arrest their attention. We have to use every device possible to reach them and to teach them, and we need not be so apologetic about entertaining them. I mean, they've been entertained all week long, every time they turn around. I have no apology for putting a good singer in front of them to entertain them if they're not Christians; you've got to do something to reach them.

I think you're really hitting the nail on the head, and those people who are there during the Easter season are there probably more out of obligation than inspiration, granted. But if you're up there speaking about where they live—about failures, about death, and about futility—you're going to connect with some of them.

Interviewer: What are some of the methods you find yourself using in trying to arrest their attention?

Lucado: I'm a big storyteller. Just yesterday in our church I told a story for the whole sermon. I wrote a fable about a wise man named Shaddai who had a village full of orphans, and an orphan named Palladin who discovered that the fence surrounding the village that protected them from the wilderness had a hole in it. He discovers, after he tells Shaddai about the hole, that Shaddai himself put the hole in. So Palladin has to decide now; he's been given a choice. He can either go out or he can stay. Palladin leaves and Shaddai goes in search of him. That's a one-minute summary of what took me thirty minutes to tell. The whole thing was a story and, you know, people listened.

They love a story; they love to be captured. They're expecting me to get up and say point one, point two, point three. They're expecting all my words to rhyme and they're expecting some cute little stories—and I do that. I do that probably more

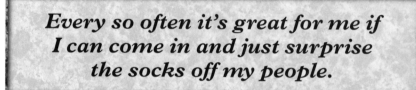

Every so often it's great for me if I can come in and just surprise the socks off my people.

than I don't do that. Every so often it's great for me if I can come in and just surprise the socks off my people, just like yesterday. I sat there in a big chair, moved the pulpit out of the way, just sat in the chair, had the opened story on my lap and just talked about it. I love stories.

It's always impressed me that Jesus told stories and didn't explain them. He'd give a parable and not explain it, with the exception of the parable of the sower and two or three others. He just told the story and left the interpretation up to the audience. Maybe he knew something more about the Holy Spirit than we do, that the Holy Spirit will make that connection with the people. There are times when our task is just to blow the dandelion fluff into the air and let the seeds fall where they may, and storytelling is a great method to do that.

Interviewer: How often would you take such an approach—where you let a story become the entire sermon?

Lucado: I will often let a story dominate a sermon. To let the story *become* the sermon, like I did yesterday, is pretty rare. I do that maybe once every four months, because I don't want to wear that out too quickly. But I will let a story dominate a point and be the main vehicle on the back of which that point rides into the hearts of people.

Interviewer: As you preach, even in your more traditional sermons, do you find yourself using a lot of narrative elements, a lot of imagery?

Lucado: I probably don't go ten minutes without an illustration, maximum five minutes. Many times I get to the church very early on Sunday mornings. My outline is prepared; it's lying there on the desk and I've prepared it such that it looks almost like a Christmas tree. It's got the main point, and then off of it I've got my subpoints, and hanging on each subpoint is an illustration. That's my decoration for the tree, and I know that if I can't articulate it, maybe a story can. If I can't get the point across, the story can. There will be many times the story will make many more points than I set out to make.

Interviewer: As you prepare to preach, do you write a manuscript and then develop your outline from that, or do you develop the outline and then preach from that?

Lucado: I develop an outline. I'll spend a day working through the text, getting the main points out of it and not being too concerned about creating the outline, just presenting it creatively, but accurately. My first goal is accuracy. Then I come in and add the creativity to it. I don't preach from an outline. By then I've worked through it enough so that it's pretty well ingrained, but I'll have that Christmas tree image in my mind and I'll work my way down the tree as I preach.

Interviewer: Easter would be an example, Christmas would be another example. There are some passages or themes that are so familiar to the average congregation that there's almost the danger of letting them become threadbare or shopworn in our preaching. Are there some particular things that you try to do to bring some freshness to those special times of the year as you preach?

Lucado: I don't know any tricks, but the longer I stay with a text, the greater the odds are I'll find something new. It's kind of like I'm looking at a piece of granite with a chisel in my hand and I'm a sculptor. If I stand there and look long enough, I'm going to see what to chip away and what's new that is going to come out.

For example, two or three Sundays ago I was preaching on what would be an Easter text, Matthew 28, it just wasn't Easter. I'd been preaching through the Gospel of Matthew and I had gotten to that point. I thought, "What am I going to say about this? I've preached this thing in and out. I'm at the bottom of it; I'm at the top of it. I know it top to bottom." But I said, "Okay, Lord, give me enough strength just to stick with it. I'm going to stare at this computer monitor and this open Bible until something connects."

Do you know what connected with me? I'd always thought that the angel came and moved away the rock so Jesus could come out. Then I started looking for that verse that says the angel moved away the rock so Jesus could come out—and it wasn't there. It occurred to me: God moved the rock so that Mary and Mary could see in. Why would he do it? Because Mary and Mary were the ones getting up early in the morning when everyone else was asleep, when everybody else was tired. Then I saw John 20:1, which says, "While it was still dark . . ." All of a sudden that took on new meaning because a lot of us are in the dark—I don't mean dark in the night, but dark in our hearts—a lot of our worlds are dark, and the hardest thing to do is to get out of bed in a dark world, to take another step, to go up to the hill.

Mary and Mary were motivated by duty. They were not walking up the hill rehearsing what they were going to say to the resurrected Lord. All of a sudden it just came to light. Here God, who had held his angels back all week long, sees these faithful, loyal disciples and he says, "I'm going to reward them. Go down there angel, move the stone away, and let them look in." Well, that didn't hit me until—I think I could honestly say four or five hours into the study, looking at commentaries, pulling them down, working through this, listening to a tape. I pulled out a tape of a friend of mine. I try anything to prime the pump.

Interviewer: You've become widely known for your books. What got you started writing, and did the books emerge out of your preaching ministry?

Lucado: Very much so. I never set out to write; I never set out to preach. I was going to go to law school and get rich. But when I became a Christian at the age of twenty-one, I became really interested in ministry and I wanted to do some foreign missions. After that I was going to come back and go to law school. I went overseas for five years, but as preparation to go, the country required two years of ministry experience. They wouldn't accept a missionary visa unless you could prove you were serious about it. Brazil required that you have two years experience.

I went to Miami, Florida, and got a job as a singles minister. They gave me the job of writing a weekly article in the church bulletin. Well, it was about a month into that job and I found myself looking forward to writing that article more than anything else. I started getting great feedback from people. Somebody said, "You ought to see if you can get these published."

By now it's time to go to Brazil. I moved to Brazil and I used my spare time to compile all of those articles into a book. I sent it to fifteen different publishers. The fifteenth said "Yes." It was called *On the Anvil,* and with it I began to learn something about the power of writing.

I don't want to chase a rabbit here, but for anybody interested in writing, I've learned, first of all, that in writing you speak to decision-makers. I'd never thought about that, but the people who take time to read are often people who are in decision-making positions. Second, when you write, you speak to people at an open moment in their lives. When I preach to the twelve hundred people in our auditorium, maybe six hundred of them really want to be there. The others—their wives dragged them along, or they are there out of habit, or they are teenagers—appear restless. At best, half of them want to be there. But when you pick up a book and read it, it's because you want to read it. You have issued an invitation and the writer is afforded a very intimate position in your day—thirty minutes, or fifteen minutes—what an honor. You're asking me to sit down and talk to you. A third advantage is that writing goes where I'll never go. I was just told that one of my books was translated into Finnish. I'll never go to Finland, but just think, someday when we get to heaven I might get to meet a guy who I encouraged along the way.

There are a lot of people who want to be writers but don't like to write. You know what I'm talking about—they want to write but don't like to because it's hard work. Like Tim Kimmel says, "Writing is like giving birth to barbed wire." It's hard work, especially that first book, because you wonder, "Is it going to be worth it?" Well, I'd like to encourage ministers who are thinking about writing, because the fact is they have more material in their files, in their minds, and in their hearts, and unless they can get it distributed it's going to die with them. If they can write it, if they can put it on paper, it's going to outlive them. A great sign of a servant is his ministry continuing after his death.

Now your second question about my sermons—my sermons dovetail directly into my writing. I work on a sermon on Monday and Tuesday and get it ready for sermon preparation. Wednesday is usually administration and counseling, but Thursday is for writing. I try to reserve Thursday to write, and I'll take the very sermon that I'm about to preach, or the one I've just preached, depending if I'm on schedule, and I'll turn that into a chapter. Even as I'm writing the sermon, I'm thinking, "When I do this in a chapter form . . ." You have to realize that in writing the eye is more discerning than the ear, so you can't have point one, point two, point three like you can in a sermon. You have to get stubbornly creative with it and craft it. It really puts much more mileage into my Sunday sermons. I have this feeling of preaching one sermon, working hours and hours and hours to get it ready, and then at Sunday lunch, I sit down and say, "All that work. It worked once, but I'll never see it again." If you can put it into a manuscript, then a sermon has unlimited potential.

Interviewer: How far ahead do you work, since you're doing both preaching and then manuscript preparation? How far ahead do you plan your preaching schedule so that it ties in and relates?

Lucado: I am learning to do this better. There was a time when I barely planned three or four weeks in advance, sometimes only one week in advance. But I preach expositionally through a book. For example, in September I preach Colossians, and I'll finish Colossians in mid-February. Barring any major interruptions—which we're absolutely certain there will be—I pretty well know where I'm going with it by mid-February, when my task will be to get it into manuscript form and to the publisher by April.

I am learning to plan ahead. Our music minister really appreciates that. The educational people really like that a lot better, and the worship people like that. I've been reluctant to do it, but I'm learning.

Interviewer: What suggestions would you make to a pastor who is interested in publishing sermons?

Lucado: The key in writing is to not sound like a preacher. If people pick up the book and start reading and it sounds like a sermon, they're going to put it down. Beyond that, I don't really know what to say. I don't know how to do it. I've never taken a creative writing class. I've never attended one and I'm never going to teach one. It just kind of happened with me, but sometimes it doesn't happen. My editor will tell me—she'll write it in big letters on the manuscript—"Sounds like a sermon." I'll go back in and try to pull out all of the sermonic feel.

There's just something about a sermon that doesn't write well and there's something about a chapter that doesn't preach well. These are two different tasks. For example, a chapter has one

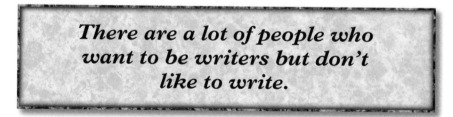

There are a lot of people who want to be writers but don't like to write.

point; a sermon can afford two or three—even though I know we're supposed to really focus in on one—but a chapter cannot. If it does, you're going to wear out your reader. You have to have one clear point which you come at from four or five different angles.

It's great for a chapter to major in word crafting—doing things you can't do in preaching unless you just read your sermons; if you try to craft a sermon to an infinite detail, it gets sluggish. So, they're two different crafts. All I get from the sermon is two or three good illustrations and the key point. I have to throw out several good points. I just can't get them into the sermon, and so I'll have to pick out one key point and focus in on that and then select my illustrations. The rest goes out.

Interviewer: What do you see as the direction of your preaching over the next several years?

Lucado: First of all, I want to find some way to really amaze people with Jesus Christ. Our goal is that when they stand up and walk out they're saying, "What an incredible Savior," not, "What a great sermon," or, "What a great church." So I am constantly looking for ways to tell people in creative ways how great Christ is. I grew up with some of the kindest, most gracious preachers in western Texas, but they were so boring, so dull. Even as a teenager I was thinking, "I could do better than those guys." I really believe that my task is to keep my church's attention whatever it takes. That's my task. They're gracious enough to come to listen. It's my task to be prepared to speak. I don't really have a larger direction than that. That might be as large as you can get.

Interviewer: Are there some things that you would encourage young preachers to do?

Lucado: Three things: One, always have a Bible study going with a non-Christian, always be in touch with non-Christians. We have a Wednesday night Bible study in our house that's an outreach to our neighbors, and I need to do that. If I don't, I'll forget where the unbelievers are, because I'm surrounded by believers. My secretary is a believer, my staff are believers, my custodian's a believer, my dog's a believer.

Second, have one ongoing counseling relationship, and note I said *one,* because most of us who are preachers—this is contrary to what I was taught—most preachers are not good counselors. In a day when therapy has reached the point that it has, we're good listeners, but most people need good therapy. If we're in relationships with people who need therapy and all we're doing is listening, they're just going to take up our time.

So I need two people like that—one non-Christian to keep me in touch with what it's like to be lost, to hear the questions he's asking, and one hurting person to keep me in touch with pain. Now some of us don't need that. There are times in my life when I don't need somebody's help to keep in touch with pain, but as a norm I need those two people.

Third, I don't need to feel guilty about spending a lot of time working on a good sermon. At first I really felt guilty, because I didn't get out to do the hospital visitation and I didn't do the administration I thought I should. Finally I told the church, "If the sick don't get visited, tell me and I'll apologize. If the budget's not perfect, tell me and I'll do better. If you come here for several Sundays in a row and you're not challenged and encouraged with the love of Christ, you tell me and I'll resign because that's my priority."

One real practical thing helped me more than anything. When I moved to this church in San Antonio, the board of elders was going to make the decision whether I should be hired or not. I wanted to see what their priorities were, so I took twelve sets of index cards and on each card I wrote a different aspect of ministry and expectations someone would have of a pulpit minister or senior pastor, things like preaching, teaching, administration, visitation, counseling. I came up with twelve. I gave a set to each board member and I said, "I'd like you, on your own, to arrange these in priority." I was going to find out where they were. If three of them really thought I needed to be in counseling, while another three of them thought I really needed to be in preaching, while another three of them thought I really needed to be in administration, I was going to walk away from that hornet's nest—it would be an accident waiting to happen. I accepted the position because though the elders chose numbers one, two, and three in different orders, the three choices were consistent in every elder—preaching, teaching, and study. So I decided that this was where I belonged. I think that's a good way to find out the priorities of the church leadership.

March/April 1993

13

FAITHFULLY PROCLAIM THE TRUTH

John F. MacArthur

For over two decades, John MacArthur has served as pastor of Grace Community Church in Sun Valley, California. In that span of years, the church has grown from 450 to 5,000 members. Over 10,000 worshipers gather each week in three Sunday services. But his ministry has been extended worldwide through Word of Grace ministries and his radio program, *Grace to You,* now heard on four hundred radio stations coast-to-coast. Over eight million tapes of his messages have extended his ministry around the globe.

Interviewer: How would you define biblical preaching?
MacArthur: Biblical preaching is the mode of preaching in which the text of Scripture and the truths of Scripture are explained and articulated. You can go far beyond that, but biblical preaching is that which explains the Bible in terms of its text and the truths that specific text delineates.

120

Through the years, I have termed this a process of "principle-izing" the text. It's not enough to explain the text—this word means that and this word means this—unless you take the next step and draw the principle. That is theology. So biblical preaching is articulating theology in a powerful, convincing, persuasive way—that which is true about God, Christ, the Holy Spirit, man, time, and eternity.

Interviewer: How has your understanding of biblical preaching changed over the course of your ministry?

MacArthur: I don't really think that it has changed. When I began my ministry at Grace Community Church twenty-two years ago (and this is the only church I have pastored), my goal was to exegete Scripture—not for the sake of exegesis, but for the sake of eliciting out of the text the truths that God put in Scripture and then pounding those truths into the minds of the congregation through a powerful communicative process. That hasn't changed at all. My study habits haven't changed, nor has my approach. I certainly know more now—the well is a little deeper—but I can honestly say that my theology has not changed.

But this is also true—people seem to have an increasing tolerance for that kind of preaching in many circles. I can trace certain trends and a visible process over the past twenty-two years. When I first came to this church as pastor, I started to preach this way and people flooded the place. It was an interesting time. It was just after the publication of The Living Bible, for what it's worth, and that certainly gave people a fresh insight into Scripture. Then came the New American Standard Bible, the Jesus Movement, Calvary Chapel, and the intensive interest in personal Bible study. People came to church carrying Bibles with covers featuring a dove and a cross, and all that. Christian bookstores and publishers began to flourish. Maranatha Music hit, and Christian music exploded.

I really think that one hundred years from now the '70s and the early '80s will look like a revival, and that period really was. There was a tremendous hunger for the Word of God, a tremendous interest in expository preaching, a tremendous and fresh new interest in doctrine. We began to teach, and it was in demand. Our church exploded and grew. People wanted me to speak here and there and everywhere.

I'm saying the same things now I was saying then, but the climate is so different that I am now a problem in some circles. I am not doing anything differently, but we have gone through that revival and now, on the other side, we find ourselves in a media approach to the church—a pragmatic kind of approach in which the church is focused on marketing strategies and all that kind of thing.

We have thrown the door open to every kind of theology. We want to embrace everybody, and that leads to a low level of tolerance for those who resist the embrace. I have lived through this transition. What I do isn't different, what I say isn't different, but the climate is *very* different.

Interviewer: You say that your study habits have not changed. Just how do you get from text to sermon and how do you prepare your messages?

MacArthur: I generally preach through books of the Bible, with an emphasis on the New Testament. Early on, I felt that the Lord wanted me to focus on the New Testament, so I went to college and took four years of Greek and three more in seminary.

The goal I set for myself when I entered the ministry was to preach expository messages through the entire New Testament, which I am still trying to do. With this method, I always know where I am. I take up a unit of thought, a paragraph, and I know every week where I'm going to go. Through that process, I will be introduced to themes in my study that will launch me off on a special series of topics, but they are almost always connected to the text. What I basically do is spend Wednesday, Thursday, and Friday of every week in preparation, and I still do that. I did it in my early years, and I am still at it three days a week. It takes a day and a half for the morning sermon and a day and a half for the evening message.

I start by reading the text. I know what is coming, because I am preaching contextual messages. I have anticipated its content. I take the text and read it repeatedly so that I have it clearly in mind, and then I begin to view things through the text. When I hit Wednesday, I go to the original language and really dissect the text so I know what I am dealing with. I want to know what it says. That's really what I am after: What does the text say?

I want to make sure that I have dealt with all the problems, all the issues, all the grammar, all the syntax, all the word study or whatever is involved. Then I take a pad of paper and copiously take down all that data. By then I really have a feel for that unit of Scripture in its context.

From there, the second step is for me to expose myself to commentaries, taking advantage of past illumination so that I don't reinvent the wheel. I enjoy commentaries because they give me a sense of how the text has been interpreted within a range of theological frameworks. These are helpful, whether they are coming from hardline Calvinism, all the way over to Arminian, sacramentalist, or other systems. I enjoy a breadth of exposure to commentaries because I get a feel for how other theological systems have interpreted the text.

I rarely read other books on a given text because I am looking for context, but once in a while I will. I might read through fifteen commentaries. Then, if I come across a special book or journal article on that text, I will get that as well. All of that data goes into the grist.

By the time I have framed a main idea, a main proposition that I will build the sermon around, the text begins to fall into a sequential pattern. That structural pattern, a series of points, is the third step in the process. That's when I refine it down to what I want to say. The last thing I do is put in illustrations. I primarily use biblical illustrations, those which come directly from other biblical texts. I do this for several reasons. One, they not only add interest, but also bring authority. Two, they teach as they illustrate. Three, they continue to familiarize the congregation with texts throughout Scripture.

Interviewer: You are not hesitant to direct the congregation to the text—and to keep them in the text.

MacArthur: No, not at all. In fact, that's the key to my preaching. I keep them ever in the text. I have found that it's much easier for the congregation to follow me if I stay in the text than if I walk around it.

It is also vitally important that they have a sense of adventure. There is a sense in which they must know that I cannot tell them everything about this text. They must expect the text to unfold and explode in their own minds at some point. With every text, they should know that there is something beyond the obvious. If the hearers are not really in the text, they will not be able to see it. I am not going to berate what is obvious. I'm not going to hammer away at what they can read for themselves.

You know, the average expository preacher I hear reads the text, states the obvious, and tells stories about it. But the text holds some truths and meaning that the average layperson does not have the tools or the time to draw out. I need to unfold those things in a way that will excite the hearer—at least that's the goal. I keep them in the text with the promise that something is going to unfold—something very, very important that they will miss unless they are with me in the text.

I set the address repeatedly. That is, I refer time and again to chapter and verse. I also repeat where we have been. "Now remember, we said *this*, and then we said *this*, and now we are saying *this*." The persons sitting in the congregation tune in and tune out—that is a part of the hearing process. If they tune back in and can't find where we are in the text, they become frustrated because they have lost the context. So I repeat where we are throughout the sermon, hopefully enough times to pull them back in again and get them back into the flow.

Interviewer: How foreign is the biblical world to the average resident of southern California? How do congregations respond to expository preaching in an age when they no longer recognize much of the Bible?

MacArthur: Well, the biblical world is exceedingly foreign to southern California, and to America as a whole. There is no religious tradition. People would say to me, "You know, you are completely unrealistic in attempting to do expository preaching in the southern California context. Everybody's into relationships, into making their world more comfortable, and you are completely out of touch!"

Our experience at Grace Community Church has proven that advice to be absolutely opposite to the truth. The more faithfully we exposit the Word of God, the more powerful our ministry becomes—and we watch that happen week after week after week.

We have a baptism service every Sunday night, and we baptize from five to twenty people each week. Some of this comes from listening to expository preaching, but most of it is due to the fact that our people are strong in the Word and in the Lord, so they reproduce themselves. We believe that the church is gathered together for worship and then scatters to evangelize. In truth, I am not attempting to preach to the unregenerate southern Californian. I'm working to build up a church and let the church multiply. Unbelievers come to Christ every week.

Interviewer: Give us a brief sketch of the history of Grace Community Church.

MacArthur: The church is now thirty-five years old, and I have been pastor there for twenty-two years. Grace Community Church was founded by a Methodist who had been associate pastor of another church in the San Fernando Valley. He died of a heart attack and was followed by a Baptist. He also died while pastor of the church. Neither of those pastors had made enough out of theology to make any difference apparent.

At that time the church was a strong, young church in a strong, young community. They were reaching kids through a very aggressive youth ministry and the church was full of young people. When I became pastor in February 1969, the church had about 450 members but it was alive and vibrant. The church had acquired property in a very good location and it had a good profile with great visibility.

So I came when the church was thirteen years old. My goal was not really to build a church. I didn't have that kind of desire. My first goal was not to lose the people who were there! When a new pastor comes, it is often followed by a bunch of people leaving. I said, "Lord, just keep them here." It was a sovereign situation.

There were certain factors at work which made what I was doing particularly on target. The greatest of these was the new interest in Bible study coming out of traditional Christianity. All of a sudden people were reading the Bible, and they wanted to know what it meant. The youth movement and the Jesus Movement had both taken place, and there was a tremendous enthusiasm and openness about the Christian faith.

The church just took off and doubled every two years for about eight years. It went to eight hundred, then to sixteen hundred, then to thirty-two hundred at just that kind of pace. There was no advertising, no promotion, lousy music; nothing but an incredible appetite for the teaching of the Word of God.

I would also add that I have pastored four churches in one place. The first church was that 450-member congregation, which then exploded and grew. It was an exciting place where you couldn't do anything wrong. The second church was the big church that eventually arose. People were coming in who had no experience of the growth, very little understanding of what we had been through, and they expected everything to be perfect.

The third church came in the late '80s, when God seemed to take his hand of blessing off of the congregation. It was a very trying time. We are now in the fourth church, which is in a euphoric period of unbelievable growth. I am one of the few guys who finds out what is on the other side of that experience with church number three!

Interviewer: Are you saying that the grass is sometimes greener in the same place—only later?

MacArthur: Exactly. Church number four is like spring. I think churches have seasons. We went through winter and this is spring again and everything is growing. I see the sovereign hand of God at work. We had nothing to do with it when it was growing, and I don't think we had anything to do with it when we were being tested. I think it was God's purifying hand doing his work.

Interviewer: We live in a society which rejects the theological, and the church has increasingly joined the secular resistance. You have been a voice crying in the antitheological wilderness. How do you see the present challenge?

MacArthur: Today's climate is almost antidoctrinal. I just completed a series of sermons on spiritual discernment, trying to attack the very obvious lack of discernment in the churches. Not only is the church not discerning, it is increasingly hostile to anyone who is. It sees anyone with discernment as a threat to unity and love.

I made this statement in those sermons: The evangelical church would never buy liberal theology. But the Enemy knew that, and so he has sold us a bill of goods in liberal hermeneutics. Unchecked, we will fall into liberal theology. That's the frightening reality of it all—the hermeneutic of love and acceptance and unity destroys all discernment.

One very well-known preacher took me out recently and said, "Your books are divisive." My response was, "Of course they are—that's not news. If you take a strong stand on an issue and

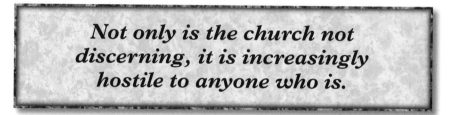

Not only is the church not discerning, it is increasingly hostile to anyone who is.

you take a firm conviction doctrinally, you have just divided." Some will stand on one side and others on the opposite side. But there is very little tolerance for that.

It is a great concern to me that the evangelical church is marked by such a lack of theological preaching, which results in a lack of discernment. This uneducated sort of theologically illiterate congregation can be led astray by every element of Satan's cunning and craftiness.

Interviewer: That lack of discernment has led Christians into an open embrace of the "self movement"—psychologies, theologies, and practical models which revolve essentially around the self as the source of all meaning and significance.

MacArthur: That's why I wrote my book *Our Sufficiency in Christ.* If you really pin me to the wall, I must say that the three issues I dealt with in that book have virtually devastated the church. I don't think we begin to realize just how bad our current situation is until we detect how little interest there is in pursuing Christ, like Paul wrote about in Philippians 3. There Paul is writing about pressing toward the mark, and that mark is Christ and Christlikeness—and that was everything! The church has largely abandoned that.

Psychology is, by definition, humanistic, evolutionary, and atheistic. It developed as an alternative to Christianity as a way of explaining human problems. I sat recently with a prominent Christian psychologist and asked him, "What part does psychology play in sanctification?" There was no answer. It plays no part—it can't. If it has no part in sanctification, then what is its purpose in the life of a Christian?

You often hear, "Well, some people can't get sanctified because they have psychological problems that must be removed before they can start the process." That is *horrendous* theology—an absolutely unbelievable theology which says that God can do his work only after a good therapist has jump-started the patient. The fact that the church has bought into that kind of thinking is mind-boggling.

I must compare this to the situation in the Soviet Union, where I have been doing a great deal of work. There is no interest in this kind of "self" psychology over there. The Soviet church has experienced years of total persecution. In the United States, we are consumed with artificial problems—"I don't like my nose," or, "I don't like the way someone treats me"—all this cosmetic kind of stuff. We have really cheapened ourselves.

The issue of pragmatism has also brought a host of problems, the idea that you must *market* the church. And mysticism is still around. In the history of the church, mysticism is old hat, but it is still here in the idea that truth somehow rises up from within a person through an individual's own spiritual experiences. What really frightens me is that the church has bought into this all over again, and if you say anything against it, you are looked at as unloving and divisive. You don't deal with the issue; you simply castigate the criticism as divisive.

Interviewer: And the worldview you describe is often brought to church by people looking for the preacher to render nothing more than therapy. How does the preacher—who has the inescapable responsibility to expound the Word of God—address people who come to church hoping to leave feeling better about themselves?

MacArthur: Let me put it this way: If you are driving down Roscoe Boulevard and you saw our church, you would feel good about it, because the grass and the flowers and the landscaping are so beautiful. The church has been awarded a Valley Beautiful citation, because we believe that God is a God of beauty and his people ought to take care of things to reflect this conviction.

When you come in the church campus, you'd meet some very nice people who are hosts and hostesses. They would take you to your place and make you feel warm and welcome. When you enter the sanctuary, you would hear a great orchestra and wonderful music.

You would be feeling very good—until I get up to preach. As soon as I get up, that good and comfortable feeling will disappear, because my goal in preaching is to confront you with what God has to say about life. For all of us, that is convicting. I don't have the goal of making these people feel good, to try to fix their problems in life. I believe that you live out your theology. Theology becomes the controlling factor in all of our relationships. So my goal is to get them thinking rightly about God, his blessings, and his demands.

Interviewer: How should the preacher measure effectiveness and faithfulness in the pulpit?

MacArthur: Well, I think there is only one genuine measuring standard. First, I must measure my own life before God. I must first of all be a man of God. What I say is the overflow of who I am. I will never be powerful in the pulpit if I am not speaking out of the vortex of a dynamic relationship with the living God. That is where it starts.

The measure of my ministry is this: Was I a steward of the mysteries of God? Did I guard the treasure so that from the beginning to the end of my life I kept the purity of truth? Did I faithfully proclaim the truth as it should be proclaimed? Those are the marks of a faithful steward.

I am so passionately burdened not to misinterpret Scripture. I am driven by my understanding of Scripture. It drives everything in my life, because I take the psalmist's statement to be true when he said in Psalm 138:2, "For you have exalted above all things your name and your word." Nothing is more precious to God than his Word, and every time I interpret a passage, I exercise a sacred trust. I'm driven by that, compelled to be a steward of that treasure and to regard it with all the faculties and spiritual resources that I have.

Interviewer: What is your exhortation to fellow preachers?

MacArthur: I can't do any better than Paul: "Preach the Word; in season and out of season; reprove, rebuke, and exhort with all longsuffering." If you understand that verse, you understand the ministry. The Word—preach it! Be quick to preach the Word whether it seems appropriate or not. The culture will tell you that it is inappropriate and that it doesn't matter, but preach the Word.

The essence of that preaching is reproof, rebuke, and exhortation. People will not always like it, but that is what will transform their lives. Don't succumb to those people looking for teachers who will tickle their ears, make them feel good, and raise their self-esteem. They are seeking a diversion from the gospel.

When you preach the Word with faithfulness, you can say with Paul, "I don't have to worry about going to face my Lord. I'm ready because I have been faithful to his charge." The measure of your ministry is the truth of your preaching and your faithfulness to guard the treasure and pass it on.

November/December 1991

PREACHING WILL NEVER LOSE ITS POWER

James Earl Massey

For over three decades, James Earl Massey has captivated congregations and fellow preachers through his preaching and teaching. Recently retired as dean of the school of theology and professor of preaching and biblical studies at Anderson University, Massey first gained a national reputation as pastor of Detroit's Metropolitan Church of God—a pulpit he held for twenty-nine years.

Later, he served as international radio preacher for his denomination and as dean of the chapel at Alabama's famed Tuskegee Institute. He is a charter member of *Preaching*'s board of contributing editors.

With an air of distinct graciousness and a voice of Christian conviction, Massey is an effective and faithful servant of the Word.

Interviewer: How do you define Christian preaching?
Massey: Christian preaching is the kind of statements, based on New Testament teachings, which highlight the ministry of

131

Jesus Christ in his relation to human need. Although I believe in sermons about God, which can broaden our understanding of our Creator and the One by whose providence life is ordered, I think the Christian note in preaching is different than the accent on God alone.

I make a distinction between preaching about *God* and preaching about *Christ*. I do believe that the preacher who takes God seriously must finally move to the New Testament, teaching about God in Jesus Christ—even if only to understand how God has made himself known through the Son. Yet there are those who preach only about God and not about Jesus the Christ. Their understanding of Jesus as Son will have to wrestle with the whole New Testament notion of Jesus as Savior. Christian preaching has to deal with that esoteric element in our Lord's ministry.

Interviewer: How do you view this as a problem in the contemporary church? Do you think that this is a particularly modern problem?

Massey: I do think this is a modern problem that is compounded by the increasing pluralism of our day. The whole notion of diversity as espoused in the seminaries has tended to level all religions in the mind of the average seminarian. Unless the professor distinctly deals with Christian particularities, the one who graduates from seminary will go out preaching *religiously,* but not *Christianly,* calling very little—if any—attention to Jesus in his salvific role.

This is one of the strong elements evangelicalism continues to insist upon. And it becomes a scandal in discussions between evangelicals and others. There are those who wish to leave matters of salvation to God and decline to deal with these from the pulpit, but the Christian preacher is under mandate from God to highlight the ministry of his Son.

Interviewer: As you think of the sermon in this Christocentric context, how does the message function within the Christian community to bear witness to Christ?

Massey: The sermon becomes, first of all, an invitational word to consider Christ. Second, the sermon becomes a means of expanding one's understanding of Christ. Sometimes the understanding must come before a decision can be reached. The sermon becomes a tool for helping a person consider Christ in the New Testament witness, and then the sermon takes on a teaching function. According to the New Testament, the preacher must be a teaching minister. The preacher has to lead the congregation to understand the meaning of Christ for all of life and to see all of life in the light of Christ. This tool we call the sermon is an invitational means, but also a means for increasing our understanding.

Interviewer: So the sermon should always place a decision before the congregation?

Massey: Yes, and I as preacher must be persuaded to act upon the information placed before me in the text. All information concerning Jesus Christ presents me with a decision. As I receive this information, I must be persuaded to act upon it. All New Testament witness concerning Jesus Christ presents implications—and I must be persuaded to act upon the implications, to trust the implications.

It is not only the preacher who must heed these implications, but all those who hear the preacher's voice. I might speak a word and lack the persuasiveness to help the person who heard me to follow through. But I must leave that in the hands of God—to send along someone else who might be able to bring that persuasion, to build upon the foundation I have made. I do not expect always to see everyone who hears me believe or accept God's Word, but at least I have done my part in getting them ready for this decision.

Interviewer: How do you prepare your preaching? Beyond that, how do you teach your students to prepare for their preaching?

Massey: Two basic ways: Either move from a human need to find what God has said with reference to that need in Scripture, or move from Scripture to that need. Whether one is sensitized by human need to move from that point to Scripture, or whether one moves from one's study of Scripture to a human need, either way God is honored and the congregation is helped.

The actual manner of preparing the sermon is a different matter, but the manner of preaching must be centered in that union between the human need and God's truth.

Interviewer: Given that union between the text of Scripture and its message regarding human need, how do you move from the text to the sermon?

Massey: I place the text at one end of an ellipse, the human hearer at the other end of the ellipse, and between the two I try to focus on the dynamic which can help the hearer to understand

> *All preaching gets us ready for Christ, introduces us to Christ, or helps us expand our understanding of Christ and relate more readily to him.*

the meaning of this for his or her life. The relation to the text in that kind of framework allows the text to open up as I see someone's face, someone's setting, situation, or need. The text opens up as I overhear what the Spirit of God is saying in that text—and throughout the whole of Scripture.

As Donald Grey Barnhouse used to say, the text should be a pivot by which the whole of Scripture bears witness. Not that I pour all of Scripture into one text, but all of the Bible that I have learned is highlighted and feeds the meaning of a particular text.

Interviewer: What is the greatest threat to genuine, authentic, biblical preaching in our own day?

Massey: There are three major threats: first, the threat of generalities, second, the threat of pluralism, and third, the threat of popularity. Generalities—trying to relate all human knowledge in such a way that we do not remain particularly Christian—level everything. The whole business of pluralism, in which we wish not to offend anyone, leads many to leave off speaking as a particularly Christian voice. The global concern of our time has opened us up to the reality of differences and to the function of those differences as valid and meaningful. But the Christian preacher must always be identified with and serve the Christian particularity.

That relates also to the third threat. When we want to be popular and please the crowds, we too often fall into generalities and avoid particularities, and therefore do not "sound the note" that we were called upon by God to keep before the public. There is a scandal of particularity to the Christian faith that is just germane to the faith itself, and apart from that, preaching has no quickening power to change human life.

You might deal religiously with any number of notions, and may even do so devotionally. You may be spellbinding in the pulpit by way of oratory and rhetoric, but the Christian has something more to say, and that is the *kerygma*. The *kerygma* takes us beyond generalities, beyond pluralism, beyond popularity, to reach to the very reason Jesus Christ came.

Interviewer: With this issue of the *kerygma*, how does one confront the kerygmatic function of the sermon in each individual message?

Massey: This becomes a problem, because in the whole range of the pastor's work, there will be times when we should deal with other important biblical concerns. That is why we pay close attention to the Christian year. Not every sermon will appear to be kerygmatic in the same sense, but all must be informed by the *kerygma* and by the realization that the *kerygma* must ultimately be served.

Interviewer: But as you acknowledge, Christian preaching, genuinely Christian preaching, *cannot* fail to be kerygmatic. The problem is that so much passes for Christian preaching these days which is, in reality, something else. The Christian preacher cannot escape Christ—and must come face-to-face with him at every issue, and in every text.

Massey: Yes, we certainly cannot escape the *kerygma*. It has to inform us always. For instance, in dealing with Psalm 139—that psalm is not explicitly Christocentric, Christ is not explicitly mentioned, but it is theocentric. Through that psalm, an individual has the opportunity to sense God's nearness to us. Those verses speak of us as "fearfully and wonderfully made," known by God within the secrecy of the womb. But this passage ultimately speaks of the love extended to us by God through Jesus Christ.

All preaching gets us ready for Christ, introduces us to Christ, or helps us expand our understanding of Christ and relate more readily to him.

Interviewer: Who have been the primary models who have helped you to develop your understanding of preaching?

Massey: There were three main models. One was my father, George W. Massey Sr. My father influenced me because of his command of Scripture. He could quote Scripture at length—so well that if you quoted any Scripture, he could tell you where you were and join you in quoting it. So I learned from my father the importance of memorizing Scripture.

The second model was George Buttrick. He was a great stimulant at the level of outlining—learning how to let the Scripture unfold logically. He helped me to sense the mood in the text and then let the sermon be shaped by that mood. Buttrick also knew how to let the text shape the structure of the sermon and serve the mood.

The third person who helped me was Howard Thurman, who modeled what I thought was an excellent devotional attitude toward God and toward the text as God's Word to us, so that the preacher becomes a worshiper along with the rest of the congregation. The preacher should not just say something to the congregation, but should respond to that pressure brought to bear upon himself or herself in the presence of God in the context of worship.

Interviewer: What do you see as the future of preaching, viewed in light of the students you see day by day?

Massey: I discern on the part of my students a strong interest in how to share Christ's Word with an aching generation. They are very much aware of the hunger of the human heart, and how little has really been done by a secular society to meet those needs.

Most of the students we now receive at the seminary are in their second careers. They are generally older than previous students, most are working, some have several degrees already. When they come to us, life has already prepared them to grap-

ple with human need—much more so than the younger seminarians. The typical student of years ago came to seminary with
a need to find out who they were. Today's student is more likely
to have that settled, and so they have a strong sense of dedica-
tion to get about the business.

Interviewer: You have taught and influenced thousands of
preachers through your teaching, preaching, and writing. What
is your word to your preaching colleagues—partners in the service of the Word?

Massey: Preaching as God intended it will never lose its power
nor its reason for being. Human concern will shift with every generation, but God's means of addressing human need will never
change. So to find out how God has moved in history and to be
open to follow that path is to remain relevant. Outside of that path,
there is no relevance, even if there is, for a time, attractiveness.

The only path of success in God's eye is for us to follow what
he has mandated for us to do. And that mandate, as spoken
through his servant Paul, is to preach the Word, in season and
out of season.

September/October 1992

15

THE POWER
OF COMMUNICATION

─────────────

Calvin Miller

Calvin Miller has been called the poet laureate of American evangelicalism. Known to many through his poetry and other literature, Miller is also an accomplished preacher. During his tenure as pastor of Omaha's Westside Church, he led the small church's growth to more than seven thousand members. Now he serves as writer-in-residence and professor of communication studies at Southwestern Baptist Seminary in Forth Worth, Texas.

A *Preaching* contributing editor, Miller delivered the prestigious Mullins Lectures on Preaching at Southern Baptist Theological Seminary in 1988. His thoughts on preaching found expression in those lectures and in his books *Marketplace Preaching* and *Spirit, Word, and Story: A Philosophy of Marketplace Preaching.*

Interviewer: I am taken with the description you gave of preaching at the onset of *Spirit, Word, and Story.* You described

138

preaching as "glory made wise with compassion." How did you arrive at this memorable and vexing phrase?

Miller: Well, I started with Paul's definition of preaching as foolishness. The older I get, the more I respect the sermons of those who have been in the ministry for a long time, have struggled with their churches, have struggled as students and scholars preparing sermons each week, and who, as they struggle physically, spiritually, and intellectually, really gain a "second sight."

I was with Ray Stedman recently, and he has been at Peninsula Bible Church in Palo Alto for almost thirty-five years. He preaches in a Bible church, with all that mystique. He really is what I would be lobbying for, a great illustrator with a balance between precept and story. He talks about what the years in the pulpit have taught him. I enjoy John Killinger for much the same reason. Something happens when preaching grows wise. That takes some time, but it does add glory to preaching.

Interviewer: As you say this, you have been at Westside Church for almost twenty-four years. That is a remarkable fact in this day of short-term pastorates. Has this brought a tinge of glory to your own ministry?

Miller: Well, you can always brag about being in one place for so long, but if you get confessional, there are many times when you would have left, due to the pain that can come in those years. The ministry is always somewhat like a roller-coaster. There are peaks and valleys, seasons of pain and great seasons of celebration. A twenty-four-year perspective reveals more seasons than daily changes. But in all of these seasons you go on studying, struggling, and you go on preaching. I admire younger preachers, but there is something about the wisdom of the years.

Interviewer: Time is obviously very important to you. You speak very reverently of the preacher's gift of time.

Miller: We have to number our days. We must take the time to plan our preaching. I look after the Christmas season and all of the pageants and see a couple of weeks and an opportunity for planning my preaching so that it fits the needs of the congregation. There is a time to plan and a time to preach, but reflection allows me to use the time when time will get short. And time *will* get short. That must always be on the preacher's mind.

Interviewer: You also speak in a different light of the gift that the congregation makes in worship; a gift of time as well. That gift is not to the preacher, but to God, and yet the preacher stands as the steward of that gift.

Miller: I think this is one of the greatest dangers of the pulpit—to waste the hearers' time. If you waste thirty minutes of one thousand people's time, you have wasted five hundred human hours. That is a sin. We must be good stewards of this gift of time. This is one reason I always stress preparation—and even some attention to a manuscript as a part of preparation. There is no use for wax in the pulpit. A preacher who preaches for forty-five minutes or more may well have a good bit of wax in his sermon.

Interviewer: You are an advocate of one element which is often missing from evangelical discussions on preaching—mystery. You go so far as to speak of "the imperative mystery of preaching." How did you discover this imperative element?

Miller: You know, Urban Holmes helped to open my eyes to this in *The Future Shape of Ministry,* and he introduced me to Theodore Roszak's definition of the preacher as shaman, that luminal figure through which strange powers seem to play. Worship requires mystery, whether it starts in a trumpet solo or in a prayer. The Spirit of God can bring about these graced moments, which can only be explained in terms of mystery, and not logic. The sermon is dropped down into that mystery.

Interviewer: You organized your philosophy of preaching around the three elements of Spirit, word, and story. How did you arrive at this structure?

Miller: Well, as I began to write the book, I saw it as a textbook on preaching, but the more I thought about it, what I was really dealing with was a philosophy of preaching. Other writers give attention to this, but the elements of Spirit, word, and story became my concern. Too little attention has been given the synergy between these elements. The older I get, the more I see preaching in terms of worship. Worship will be the great word in the '90s. This requires a real synergy in worship between Spirit, word, and story. When that synergy happens, there is more there than the sum of those parts.

Interviewer: The Holy Spirit has been described as "the neglected member of the Trinity," yet you began with the Spirit as your first consideration.

Miller: I don't know how to explain this fully, but I find that my own walk with Christ—when I know myself best in what I talk about as "the table of inwardness"—is an experience with the Spirit. I am nourished by the mystical devotional literature. I don't find many evangelicals talking about this, but something happens when we read this wonderful literature and discover a new walk with Christ. They know something of what I mean about the preacher as shaman—and yet a human. People want you to be human, but there is something about the preacher enriched by sharing this mystical experience—something more than the didactic.

Interviewer: The turn to narrative is one of the great characteristics of our day. You are a champion of story preaching over what you term precept preaching, a more didactic style. Most evangelicals were raised with precept preaching and often see it as a norm. How did you come to turn to story preaching?

Miller: You know, I was only tempted to preach precept sermons for about a year. It was when I began at Westside. I was influenced by some precept preachers, and so I went in that direction. I had an overhead projector and handed out extensive outlines each Sunday. I finally came to say, "Miller, that's just not

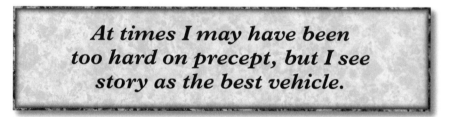

> *At times I may have been too hard on precept, but I see story as the best vehicle.*

who you are." There are some who can do it well, and for whom that is a natural style, but it was not me. The style has to be native to the preacher.

Interviewer: Doesn't the style have to fit the congregation as well? Some congregations can follow narrative more readily than others, and some are more effectively reached by precept.

Miller: I really think that story is the better way to go. I try to intersperse the epigram and the proverb along with the narrative flow. You are right, of course. There are congregations naturally drawn to story preaching and others to precept sermons. There is a natural balance there. At times I may have been too hard on precept, but I see story as the best vehicle.

Interviewer: To be fair, you do suggest that story and precept should work hand in hand. Are you careful not to draw an absolute line at narrative?

Miller: David Buttrick's *Homiletic* has recently helped me at this point. I think the notion of moves and structures, where the story provides the moves and precepts provide structure, is a good way to see the process. I go through my sermon and want to be sure that I label the key things that I do not want to miss. I want to move the hearer along. I may have twenty different moves along the way—illustrations, points, precepts, whatever—but it is usually carried along by the story.

Interviewer: Why is precept preaching so popular among Protestants and especially, perhaps, among evangelicals?

Miller: For one thing, precepts don't take as much work with the sermon as a carefully crafted story. Stories are work, and effective storytelling takes experience, innate gifts, and hard work. The really good storytellers hone their craft over a lifetime; they are always working on it. Some preachers are not willing to work at this, and others may not believe that they have the gifts. It can be intimidating, and some people probably shouldn't move into story as a primary method.

Interviewer: Does a turn from precept sermons run the danger of losing the doctrinal content of preaching? Is story suitable for preaching on doctrinal issues?

Miller: That is always the argument against story, but I always go back to the fact that the Bible is basically a narrative—many little stories in the context of *the* story. Here and there the stories crystallize into precepts, or precepts may precede the stories, but it is very hard to say that the Ten Commandments are strictly precept. You cannot separate them from divided seas and descending manna, for that is their milieu. That's how they come to be. This can be a losing game. Both precept and story have their place, and the preacher can find a natural balance.

Interviewer: In your book *The Empowered Communicator,* you identify seven keys to gaining and holding an audience with preaching. Tell us about those keys and why they're important.

Miller: I actually think of the seven keys as connections between listener and speaker. They encompass some very practical things and are very simple little things. They don't come so

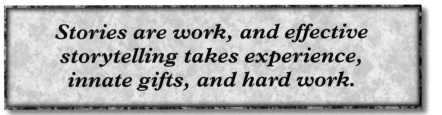

Stories are work, and effective storytelling takes experience, innate gifts, and hard work.

much from the world of homiletics as they do from communication theory, and I think that may be a strength in the book's plea to move preaching more in the direction of what a secular speaker has to do to be heard and accepted.

When I've done seminars on this, I've tried to describe how uncomfortable we would feel if Bill Clinton used the rules of homiletics in a national address, in terms of breaking down a word study or setting out points—that would sound odd. I think that today's listener is nourished on contemporary secular models. More and more that is going to require us to be speaking with the same kinds of rules in mind.

The keys are very simple things. The first key is to build a relationship. I think it's the first time a book on the sermon talks about the speech before the speech, consciously separating what you need to say first to get their attention from what you've actually come to say. The second key is the ego barrier—in the first three minutes you give the people the sense that you are there on their behalf, and you make them believe it. The third key is promising hearers that you have usable information to give, making them a promise, and keeping that promise with your content.

The fourth key is tension and resolution. I illustrate it with a situation in Nebraska about slipping on the ice in winter. When you first feel yourself beginning to fall, for a few seconds your every nerve is focused on how you're falling, what's happening as you fall, and when in God's name will your fall be over—there is nothing relaxed about your person. Everything is in tight focus. When you finally hit the ground, you may break something, it may hurt, you may be embarrassed that others have seen you—but at last it's over. So we want to create this same kind of irresolution. We're trying to build, in this fourth key, that kind of tension where every nerve is focused.

Key five is constructing a pyramid of priorities. To me, that's really important. I go back and pick up the old idea of character. Three phases exist in a pyramid of priorities, and the first of them is truth—every preacher has to tell the truth. The next phase up from that is for preachers to tell the truth with interest—interest others in their truth. And the third and most glorious phase comes after they have told the truth and have interested others; now they inspire and quicken and challenge people in an excited way. Truth, interest, and inspiration are the phases of those priorities.

Key six is making sure they hear with all kinds of audio values. And here I deal with a bunch of things that are so important in terms of techniques—the microphones, the lighting, the things that really make a person heard and seen.

Finally, key seven talks about what you do when you sense communication failure even as you preach or speak. I think all of us have had the experience of watching ourselves fail and not knowing what to do to correct our communication while we are

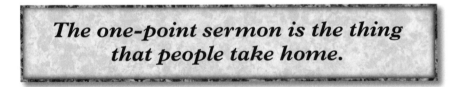

The one-point sermon is the thing that people take home.

failing. So I have some suggestions to regain a failing speech. Of course, sometimes a communication that's failing as we deliver it cannot be redeemed; in those cases I've got some advice on how to quit early, and how important it is to quit early. Nobody ever got mad because the preacher quit early.

I've put those seven short things together to show how you succeed at keeping attention.

Interviewer: In your book you talk about the one-point sermon. How does that differ from more traditional sermon structures?

Miller: The one-point sermon is the thing that people take home; they know that single point without looking at what they've written in their Bibles or the sermon outline sheet you gave them when they walked in the back door. In other words, what point do they remember, what was the point of that sermon? You may have two or three ideas that serve to focus and make that one point solid, but if you've consciously given the audience three sermonettes, even under an alliterative outline, every time you add another point you think is important you divide the attention the audience is able to give and the memory with which they are able to retain your point.

The sales director comes to the sales force and says, "This week we're going to go out into the community and we're going to sell pipe wrenches." He gets them all excited, all whipped up, and they all go out and sell pipe wrenches. Next week they come back and he says, "You did so well with pipe wrenches last week that this week we're going to sell two things, pipe wrenches and peanuts. Peanuts are fundamental to human happiness and people need peanuts just like they need pipe wrenches." No matter how hard he exhorts this effort, he divides the urgency with which they saw the single vision.

Never let yourself try to sell two things at one time. And if you try to sell three points, just remember that each time you add another product to the line, you divide the urgency with which they would have seen the one point of the communication.

Interviewer: It sounds as if the one-point sermon is what might otherwise be referred to as the sermon's central truth—that key idea on which everything focuses.

Miller: Right. I call it the sermon logo. Al Fasol, a colleague of mine, calls it the focal point. The idea is the same. I say in my book that I think the classic people who have done this are America's great Black preachers. They have been able somehow to sell one thing and to repeat it with a kind of planned redundancy—an ingenious and creative redundancy—that quickens that same, simple, single idea again and again.

Interviewer: You are a preacher, poet, and novelist. How do these lives intersect with and support one another?

Miller: I used to wonder. I don't so much anymore because every great homiletician these days is making a plea for narrative. People like Haddon Robinson will talk about not just telling a story, but preaching in pictures. So in a video-oriented generation, I think novels succeed if they create strong images. In fact, when there are fifty thousand new novels every year—as there are in our culture—the real question is whether plots are very important. Maybe what's really important are the pictures of people—the characterization and the images with which you speak or preach.

I think novelist and preacher fit very well together. I wish I could make preachers believe, especially those who are prone to be rather left-brained, that if they would do more reading of novels to see what good writers do when they write, they could get that same kind of imagery in the sermon. I think they'd find a strong correlation of interest. So many times preachers are boring because they are not able to create the same kind of narrative power that exists in a novel.

Interviewer: Some people are natural storytellers, while others really struggle with that. In addition to reading novels, are there some other things you would encourage a preacher to do to develop that narrative side?

Miller: I do agree that some people are natural storytellers, but I don't think it matters too much. I've heard professional athletes, especially right after they become Christians, tell their story. They look down, they're weak, they use no significant adjectives, they don't know how to construct a story in any kind of literary form—they just tell what happened to them in Jesus. It's sweet and it's wonderful. They begin to cry, their lip quivers, their chin drops, and they lose control. Everything about what they do says, "This is not literary; it's not good," but there's an emotive power of the existential moment—*what happened to me* is what really communicates.

If you want to develop a narrative kind of style, try to remember that, whether right-brained or left-brained, all people have to tell somebody what's happened to them. The guy who's maybe such a jock that he's never read a novel or short story can still tell his wife what happened to him during the day. And when he's telling her, she listens. Maybe he's not a great storyteller, but he's into his story.

I think that would be a significant thing for people to understand—that stories really work in this realm not because they're told by people who know how to tell them professionally, but because, "This is my story and this happened to me." If they can pull you into that, I guarantee, storyteller or not, they will have people's attention.

I always think about the great rugby player, C. T. Studd. After his conversion, he testified in F. B. Meyer's church. Studd had that athletic shuffling of the feet, the downward look, the shyness—but he also had the immense power of just telling his story in Christ. F. B. Meyer, who was quite good at all kinds of preaching including narrative, realized that although a professional storyteller, he'd never held his people like this simple man had in telling his simple little story. He said, "You know, Studd, I'd give anything if I could hold people's attention like you just did." Studd said, "There's nothing I have that you cannot have if you're willing to be filled with the fullness of God." That may be a spiritual oversimplification, but the principle is right. If you have an experience with God, tell that experience. I think people will listen; in fact, I think it would be fascinating, and I think they're ready to hear it.

Interviewer: Perhaps a compensating factor for the lack of storytelling ability is a certain passion. Do you think that passion is lacking in a lot of preaching?

Miller: Passion is lacking. In this book and in an accompanying lecture, I talk about two things—passion and content, and I liken them to an airplane in flight. The reason an airplane flies is that its velocity exceeds its weight load. Weight load is always the content of the sermon; the passion is the velocity. If the sermon goes fast enough, if the passion is hot enough and the sermon moves fast enough, it can lift quite a bit of content. But if it doesn't go very fast, content will cause it to bog down—crash and burn, in all probability. I think you're absolutely right; I think passion is something that causes the lift, content is what delivers the payload, and that again is a matter of existence. We become more passionate about things which affect us, so what the person who wants to tell stories but thinks he or she doesn't have the ability can do is to somehow say, "This is my story." You cannot tell your own story without being peculiarly involved and passionate about it. Tell those kinds of stories.

That's where I would differ a little bit from David Buttrick in *Homiletic*, who says to not get yourself involved in your illustrations. I don't believe that. I think illustrations with the most passion are the ones that happen to us. We always tell those with passion.

Interviewer: What do you think is the greatest challenge facing preaching and preachers in the '90s?

Miller: I think the number one, all-time greatest challenge is to communicate usable information in the sermon, while at the same time being sure that our preaching is saturated in biblical truth. If we give usable information without the Bible, we abandon the next generation; the church will not exist long. I truly believe it's the number one challenge, and I find very few preachers who do it very well. The number one spokesperson on this has been Elizabeth Achtemeier. Again and again, she cries out for a textual sermon that bears usable information. That is the challenge of modern sermons.

Interviewer: Why do you love preaching?

Miller: I ask myself that. Somehow I can't stay away from it. I'm drawn to do it. I'm scared to death of it. But there is an elixir, an addictive need in my life to talk to people and have them listen to me—for us to become one. I speak in my book about the "audience lean." There are a few times in our lives when the congregation's eyes not only meet our eyes, but when their intensity so marries our own intensity that they actually lean physically toward the podium like sunflowers lean toward the sun. Those who have known that cannot live without it; you look forward to the next time. It doesn't happen all the time, but in the beginning of every speech is the possibility, "It could happen now," and that fires us into this marriage of minds.

Eric Hoffer said, "No minds are chaste, all minds copulate every time they meet." I love that electricity of intimacy of speaker and welded audience—it's a romance all its own.

There is a spiritual intimacy in preaching. I realize in many ways I'm still very big on the open public altar, the invitation. A lot of churches now are not doing it, and that's okay—every church has got to do its own thing, and I don't have any problem with that. But nothing is quite so splendid as when the Spirit of God in me reaches out and touches the Spirit of God in a listener or group of listeners, and equally splendid when that Spirit wells up in people so that there's no question that Jesus is the celebrant in the sermon and that we come together. The problem is that the "welling up" is very susceptible to be used by incipient psychotics—pastors who can "whip up" Jesus sometimes become the worst and most dangerous kind of manipulators. But if we are altruistic, it is a beautiful thing.

Interviewer: If you had the opportunity to counsel young ministers early in their ministry about preaching, what kind of counsel would you give them?

Miller: One thing I would say is never let your pulpit oratory and your parish life get separate. By that I mean that so many times people are one kind of person when they live in the parish and another kind of person when they're in the pulpit.

There's a wonderful thing that happens when we live among people. We talk to them, and the next thing you know we're in the pulpit talking—we continue talking just like we have that one-on-one relationship. In the book, I talk about the wonderful thing that happens when we consciously shrink 350 people or 150 people, 50 people or 2,000 people to a single respondent.

In summary, here's what I'd say to them: Don't ever allow the "conversational you" to get separated from the "oratorical you." The person who lives in the community is the same person who speaks in the community, and there's no difference in how you do it or the kind of rapport you feel one-on-one. Don't be a professional, be relational.

March/April 1990
and January/February 1995

16

PREACHING AND PRAYER

Ben Patterson

New Providence, New Jersey, is a long way from Irvine, California—and not just in terms of geography. Ben Patterson shifted the focus of his preaching ministry from southern California to the New York City metropolis. A popular preacher and author, Patterson was the founding pastor of Irvine Presbyterian Church in one of California's fast-growing planned communities. After a fourteen-year pastorate in Irvine, he moved to the East Coast and became pastor of the Presbyterian Church of New Providence. Currently he serves as chaplain of Hope College.

Ben Patterson is an effective and faithful preacher, who extends his preaching ministry through books such as *The Grand Essentials* and *Waiting.* He also serves as a contributing editor for *Christianity Today* and *Leadership.*

Interviewer: What kind of congregation do you see as you preach?

Patterson: It has shifted over the years. The kind of person who joined us in Irvine when we were a new church was very committed and already had some church leadership experience in another church. We had some who were seminary-trained workers in parachurch organizations in the area. They were pioneers and workers. But that has really shifted as the church has developed. We now have many who would be described as nominal Christians. I started out preaching to a very biblically literate congregation, but that has changed. Many current members are parents bringing their children to "get values." When I was preaching to the very biblically literate congregation, I could preach differently—be more challenging. I cannot assume as much now.

Interviewer: How do you define biblical preaching?

Patterson: Well, at the most basic and least imaginative level, biblical preaching is setting forth the meaning of the biblical text. The twin tasks are of taking a trip from the first century to the twentieth and back again. If the meaning is left stuck at either extreme, it isn't genuinely biblical. Biblical preaching is really setting forth the text in terms of what it meant and what it means.

Interviewer: Has your understanding of biblical preaching changed over the course of your ministry?

Patterson: Well, I don't think my understanding of biblical preaching has changed in substance, but it has changed in practice. When I preached to a more biblically literate congregation, I was much more willing to read a biblical text and take off from there, and everything I would say would flow out of the text. I could assume that most of the people sitting in the congregation were familiar with the passage, and I did not have to show them how the sermon fit the text. They were bright people, they had their Bibles open before them, and they knew what the text said.

Now I am taking greater pains, and am in a sense more conservative, in that I sound more like a verse-by-verse expositor. I sense that since the congregation is not biblically literate, they do not assume that a statement is biblical just because I said it in the course of a sermon. I want them to have the experience of having encountered the text through the sermon while they are hearing it preached. I now say, "Open your Bible and look at this," as I refer to the text.

Interviewer: The shift from a biblically literate culture to a congregation comprised of those who know very little about the

Bible at all is a challenge to almost every preacher in America. In light of that, some preachers have recommitted themselves to more structured models of biblical preaching, such as expositional sermons. Others seem to have given up on the task and preach sermons which have very little biblical content at all.

Patterson: That is an interesting development. You know, the congregation plays a part in that. During the first years of my ministry in Irvine, I took a cue from Browne Barr (a former professor of preaching at Yale Divinity School), and formed what he called a "sermon workshop." I would sit down with a group of church members and critique the sermon in terms of the text, with criteria I supplied them. That really got me plugged into what people were thinking and what issues they were dealing with. I also built up a clientele in the church who understood what I was doing in the pulpit. I later drifted away from that for a time, feeling that I had come to understand the congregation. That was probably an unfounded assumption, and I am now back at the process again. I dialogue with the group about the text—what it is about and what I am going to do.

Interviewer: How did the context of preaching in southern California shape your understanding and practice of the preaching task?

Patterson: People are always in a hurry. I tend to get a bit reactionary to that—I hope in a healthy way. When I looked out on my congregation in Irvine, I saw a group of people on their way to somewhere else—usually some kind of recreational activity which they would pursue with grim determination. Recreation is seen as a right and an "ought" in their lives. The holiness of the day is gone; there is no concept of the Sabbath. These people are rushed, and they're tired from both working and recreating. They don't even really recreate; they work at play. These people would desperately like the preacher to get the sermon done. I have reacted against that. My sermons have gotten longer and our worship services have gotten longer—and hopefully meaningfully so. We need to say, "This is one thing we are not going to rush through this week."

There are certain issues they are dealing with all the time that I find difficult to address. Many of those revolve around addiction. These people are obsessive-compulsive folks. Either we are, in reality, an addictive society, or else that is the new jargon to explain our spiritual problems. I am not sure, but addictive behavior seems to be foremost in their minds. They have high family values, but they are not mentors themselves and do not seem to have mentors like other generations have had. They are very concerned about their marriages and are confused. They feel isolated and frightened in raising their children. They do not have the institutional supports other generations had, and so they look to the church. They are looking for a parent. These concerns are behind what I see as the preaching task.

Interviewer: In your books and sermons, you demonstrate an ability to translate biblical concerns to people who do not know the stories and have not heard the texts. How do you develop the themes and issues of your sermons?

Patterson: That, in keeping with the rest of my approach, has shifted somewhat. I came into the pulpit in the mid '70s and plowed through the books of the Bible. That method was most popular in the southern California churches, which were really growing. I later became more topical—not in the older method of topical preaching, but in the sense that I have selected texts according to the topics I felt needed to be addressed. I have done this almost to a fault. But lately I have moved back to more systematic methods, sometimes using the lectionary and sometimes preaching again through a book of the Bible.

Interviewer: Is that because of your concern for the biblical content?

Patterson: Well, it goes back to the issue of biblical literacy. There are limits in looking at Sunday morning as an opportunity to *teach* something. But I want the sermon to do at least a bit of that. If nothing more, I want to get the congregation in the habit of handling the Scripture, to experience the joy of opening the Bible and letting it speak for itself. So I am disciplining myself away from topical preaching and going back to other methods. I have to say, however, that topical preaching is more popular, and even my own church members would probably wish that I did more of that. They come with questions and issues, and they want those answered right away.

Interviewer: The dynamic between human need and the demand of the text challenges every preacher who takes the task seriously. Another challenge is moving from the text to the sermon. How do you make this transition?

Patterson: That question needs to be answered at two levels—the ideal and the real. What I want to do with every sermon does not always happen. I select the texts well in advance, usually three to four months ahead. I read them devotionally first and then move to exegesis and the critical apparatus. I always do a great deal of devotional reading. Lately I have benefited greatly from praying through the text. I intercede for the church on the basis of what I see in the text. Nine times out of ten, an outline will emerge from that process. My use of commentaries and other resources is more as a check on my reading of the text. That protects my interpretation from being off the wall.

I also use my word processor and throw information into the machine, move it around, print it out, and then go to my files for illustrations and other material. One technique I have used is to get out of the church. I take all that material and go out to the park, to a restaurant, or to a shopping mall. I sit there and muse over the text. That can be remarkably helpful. All kinds of connections and anecdotes and stories come to me. Just a change of environment does that.

Interviewer: How do you develop and use your sermon manuscript?

Patterson: I always write a full manuscript and put a great deal of time and effort into that process. I rarely carry it into the pulpit. I take an outline based on the manuscript into the pulpit and preach from that. I am best when I walk into the pulpit having written a full manuscript, but with an outline in hand. I then walk into the pulpit with a combination of prepared and extemporaneous preaching. More often than not, I take to the pulpit a bare-bones outline with some notes added. I go from that blue-sky material on the text, through the manuscript, to the sermon outline. The manuscript is necessary to make that transition. It cleans up my thinking and focuses me on the text.

Interviewer: How do you connect your preaching ministry with your writing? Does your vocation as a writer assist you in your preaching?

Patterson: It really does. I started out as a preacher speaking out of an outline without having prepared a manuscript. When I listened to the tapes, I sounded unfocused and sloppy. If I write it out, my thinking is cleaner and I will come up with

> *Prayer allows me to relinquish my hold on preaching and cast myself on the mercy of God.*

better illustrations and connections. This depends on the congregation as well. My congregations have been very well educated and they appreciate the fact that I am a writer. I don't think the church I grew up in would have appreciated a pastor who was a writer, so it depends a great deal on the congregation. There are times I think that being a writer and a preacher can put me at cross purposes, because I can be so enamored with some phrase I have put together that I probably should just put it away and not think about it. That is the risk.

Interviewer: What would be your message to preachers as they are about the tasks of ministry?

Patterson: Without hesitation I would say, "Learn to pray." I think it was D. L. Moody who reminded us that Jesus taught his people how to pray, not how to preach. I guess I would rather learn how to pray than how to preach. I have a great distrust of my abilities. God has given me some abilities to communicate, and I think those gifts, taken alone, are what will thwart my effectiveness in the kingdom of God. Prayer allows me to relinquish my hold on preaching and cast myself on the mercy of God. That's when God can use me.

November/December 1990

TELEVISION
AND THE PULPIT

Quentin Schultze

Quentin Schultze has become one of the American church's most insightful observers and critics of the impact of media—particularly television—on the lives and attitudes of people. A professor of communications at Calvin College in Grand Rapids, Michigan, he has written widely about the media.

Interviewer: Television has obviously become a very pervasive influence in American culture. How has this affected the attitudes of persons who sit in the pews of our churches? Has television changed the way they think about moral and social issues?

Schultze: Television's effect on congregations, I think, falls into two major categories. One would be in how average parishioners think about their faith and about church life. Although most television drama doesn't deal very openly with the church, with clergy, and so on—religion is sort of invisible there —there's

156

a lot of religious broadcasting, and most of the religious broadcasting is watched by people who are members of churches. They are not just elderly people; some of the programs—*700 Club,* the old *PTL,* and so forth—have a significant number of younger people watching. Charles Stanley is out there with an enormous audience.

When you start looking at these biggies, what you find is that many, many people watch these programs because they think they are being fed spiritually by them in ways that they're not in their local churches. That's the rationale they give me. Now when I push it a little bit further, asking them questions about what's going on, the conclusion that I've come to is the principal effect in terms of the content of the religious broadcast is to get the congregant to think that their church somehow should match the style of what they see on TV—the style of preaching, the style of music, the pacing of the program.

It's rather an emotional and less a cerebral kind of preaching. Frequently it's an oral style of preaching—I think most good preaching is in kind of an oral style—rather than a literary style. In short, what is happening with content is that congregations more and more want their local church to be like what they enjoy from TV preaching. That's one effect.

The other effect is harder to see, but I think it's probably the biggest effect, and that is how time has been shifted in the lives of most people. Most people in North America today spend most of their leisure time watching television. There is no leisure activity that even comes close. We're talking about the average adult now, with cable and a VCR. From the figures from 1991, the average adult watches four hours and forty minutes per day of television. They're spending very little time developing relationships with people in their own family, with people in their congregations, with neighbors. So what's really suffering is interpersonal communication. When average people today come into the church, it's much more likely that they don't have a personal relationship with the people they are worshiping with, and less likely that they have much of a personal relationship with the pastor or other staff because they're not investing time in those things. So I think the body of Christ as a community is suffering significantly because of television.

The Roper studies of television, done every two years, show that if you ask people what they most want to do tonight with available time, they will say get together with family and friends—that's number one. If you then ask them what they did last night, overwhelmingly it's watch TV, so there's this tremendous need for fellowship and closeness in relationship that's simply not being met. What's happening is the congregation is becoming more and more like the TV audience—individuals in their homes, not talking together about what they're watching, not necessarily sharing much about their lives, but they're all tuned in to the same thing for a limited period of time. I think it's very hard to have a true congregation in that kind of setting.

One other effect I'll talk about briefly is the effect of the new technologies—cable, VCR, especially the remote control—on people's willingness to patiently listen and view things around them. Reflective ability, silence, meditation are all things that are disappearing in people's lives, and this affects the church significantly. People want a fast-moving liturgy and they want a pastor who has some flair in general, otherwise they become bored. This is especially true of younger people. It's much harder to get younger people excited about church, and the megachurches are growing principally on the basis of the baby boom generation. They are the ones, in fact, who are most adopting the entertainment styles into the churches, so that makes a lot of sense—they're the first generation raised on TV.

Interviewer: What about, for want of a better term, the "Murphy Brown" factor—the influence of TV on the attitudes of things like moral issues, the kinds of things that Dan Quayle was talking about? How pervasive is that in terms of changing attitudes people come to church with that may influence how they hear the message?

Schultze: Terrific question. If you asked me this question a hundred years ago, I would line up the institutions that shape someone's moral fabric as follows: (1) family, especially parents, inculcating a moral vision that they then take into the churches; (2) church; (3) schools—the order of church and school might vary a little from family to family; and (4) the media. Now we know from the studies of the younger generation—the first generation to grow up on TV and now the new technologies—that number one is the media in terms of developing a sense of morality (what morality is, what it includes, how you think about it, what kind of sensitivity you have to moral issues, and so forth). So the order would be: (1) media, followed closely by (2) the family, then (3) the schools, and then (4) the church, which is last. These are the major nurturing institutions today for moral vision and moral sensibility in our society. The person coming into church to worship is bringing along, more than anything else, a moral vision that's been nurtured by the mass media. You have to think about it this way.

The average person today in the United States and Canada is exposed to more drama on television in one year than the average person was exposed to in a lifetime prior to television. It's incredible. I believe that our moral vision is shaped, more than anything else, by the stories that we take on and put ourselves in vicariously, and preaching is to some extent making the gospel story our story. So we see ourselves in the redemptive narrative from creation, fall, salvation, second coming, and so forth. People

> *The person coming into church to worship is bringing a moral vision that's been nurtured by the mass media.*

today in most churches can't identify themselves as being in that story, even if they say they are born again. They don't quite see that they're players in God's historical movement. What are they players in? *Thirtysomething.* They're players in *Beverly Hills 90210,* which is a teenage version of *Thirtysomething.* So moral vision today is framed strongly by the media, particularly television.

Interviewer: How does a preacher adapt to that, knowing that when he sees the young adults and youth, they are coming to the preached Word with their moral values shaped by what they've seen on the tube? They are still carrying around not only *Thirtysomething* but *Leave It to Beaver* and the things they grew up on. As the preacher frames the gospel message, how does he adapt to that?

Schultze: Two adaptations are essential for preachers at this stage, I think—I'm still in process thinking about this. One is the structure of the message. I think we have to get away from literary structures which are very much linear and discursive. Point A leads to point B, leads to point C. It's like writing a lecture for a seminary professor. It's very difficult today for most people to hear that as a sermon rather than a lecture, and to be able to follow it and find it meaningful and interesting. Too many preachers have seminary professors as their principal role models, because professors are lecturing all the time. As students, they may take a course in homiletics, but they come out with all these role models of lectures, so they go into the pulpit and lecture. Well, people who are exposed to entertainment media—television for example—principally in the form of a narrative story, are not really open to a twenty- or twenty-five-minute sermon in the form of a lecture, unless you have a very academic congregation.

I think what we need to do in terms of structure, then, is to recapture an oral style of preaching. An oral style would be characterized by a single central theme. Then it would have the use of illustration, the use of example—some of them from the Scriptures themselves, some of them from real life—and so forth to build that theme. This becomes powerful. What you find interesting is that a lot of successful pastors today, without even thinking about it, are doing this. Many of them are getting away from writing out their sermons. They're going to simple outlines, or they're even throwing out outlines altogether. The preacher says, "What is the point that I want to get across? Here's the passage. How can I put this in a kind of oral style so it's me communicating with these people as if it were a conversation—so they know it's coming from someone who's grappled with this particular passage and determined the meaning of it. Here's what it means and here's how to apply it to your lives." The reason that most preaching today is better in the southern states than in the northern states is because the oral culture in the South is still stronger than in the North. The northern culture in the U.S. has been more oriented toward a kind of academic lecture—a very formal kind of style—and the seminaries tend to reflect that.

That's in terms of structure. I think it will work. It doesn't mean we need to have all kinds of visual glitz—I don't believe that for a minute. It doesn't mean you have to turn worship into a TV program with multimedia stuff and everything else.

What about content? I think the most effective content is going to be that which takes the message from Scripture and directly relates it to where people are at in contemporary culture. Prophetic preaching is that which understands how to apply the Scriptures to contemporary social and cultural situations. If people are living in the contemporary culture, and someone comes in and preaches in a way that never makes the intersection with that contemporary culture, they're lost! This means that preachers have to know enough about what's going on in the contemporary culture. They should watch *Beverly Hills 90210,* because it is the most popular program with teenagers, and there's a reason—it deals with teenagers where they're at. I don't like the answers that it provides, I don't like its overall outlook, but it's addressing the questions, concerns, and issues they have. Preachers need to know who the major role models are in the lives of young people, to know what adults are worried about and thinking about, what's going on around them, such as a lack of faith in social institutions of all kinds and in politics.

I'm not saying just come up with A and B lists of good and bad programs or films or whatever, but to understand the cultural currents and to intersect that with the gospel message. That, I think, is what really prophetic preaching is today, and it can be very powerful, very powerful. I'd like to see, for example, a sermon comparing the New Testament view of evil with the contemporary notion of evil. The notion in popular culture right now is that evil is out there, particularly in evil people who can be eliminated. That maintains our hope as a society that we can eventually get these scoundrels in jail or whatever. In fact, of course, evil is in all of us—it's part of the fall that affects all of us—and that's completely contrary to the popular culture. It's a prophetic kind of preaching to say to a congregation, "We are all sinners, and you may be doing evil things in the workplace in terms of white-collar crime, or in what you're doing in raising your family." The evidence of evil is not just out there.

Interviewer: Related to that, it seems that popular culture doesn't interpret evil nearly so much in terms of traditional moral issues as, for example, intolerance.

Schultze: Oh, yes. We let the media dictate to us as a Christian community what morality is and what scope morality includes. In fact, what I try to do in the *Redeeming Television* book is to say to the Christian community, "Our view of morality is too narrow." People say with regard to popular culture: "What about sex, violence, and profanity?" I agree those are big concerns, but we are wrong to think that those are the only concerns. There are all kinds of moral issues out there that we ought to be outraged about, but we're not because they're just not seen as the big issues. Who's going to help people think of these other kinds of issues? Racism is like a little blip on the screen now and then. It comes up because of the Rodney King beating or whatever, but this is pervasive in society. We need to address it. What about materialism? I'm a believer that materialism may be the biggest threat to the church in North America. What do we do with materialism? Television and films are filled with materialism. Look at the program *Dallas*—in some respects it was a celebration of materialism, as is much of TV. Why aren't we concerned about that? We need to define these things through prophetic preaching so that as a community we can understand what's included in morality.

Interviewer: Much of religious television has taken on the form of spiritual entertainment, as opposed to more traditional forms of preaching and worship. What are some of the factors that have contributed to that trend, and what do you see as the future place of preaching in religious television? Neil Postman says that television and preaching or worship are inherently unsuitable for one another—they just don't mix.

Schultze: I think too many preachers and theologians have bought into the arguments of Neil Postman, Malcolm Muggeridge, and to some extent Jacques Ellul, that television is an inherently evil or negative-consequence-producing media. I think this is a very wrong heading. This notion that a particular communications technology is inherently evil has been applied to every new communication technology that came along, including the book. Gutenberg's invention set a lot of people reeling. We have to see this in historical perspective.

My view is that in God's work in history, the creation unfolds, and as new technologies unfold they can be used for good or

> *Unless it's very simple preaching, it's not going to be very effective on television.*

bad, depending on whose hands they're in and what kinds of values and practices will be applied to those technologies. But—and here's the key point—no communications technology is neutral with respect to the message. None is neutral with respect to the message. Here Postman is right, here Muggeridge is right, and so forth. I think they are wrong in terms of the inherently bad influence of television and technology, but they're right that it does have its own specific thing. Every technology can communicate some things better than other things, but each has its place.

Let's talk about the place of television. Television is a medium that communicates both visually and aurally. It's not just a visual medium; a lot of people like Postman overemphasize the visual dimension of it and underestimate the aural dimension of it. It's a combination. It's a medium that is not going to trivialize everything inherently, as Postman would say—that's his basic theme in *Amusing Ourselves to Death*. He's simply wrong there. It's not like Muggeridge says, that we'll automatically communicate untruth. This is just nonsensical, but it does have its limits. I think the proper role of television for church use is in drama—because television can be a very dramatic medium—and in simple teaching. Not complex, theological teaching—you don't do advanced physics, and you don't do advanced theology through television—but simple kinds of teaching. What I would call documentary—documenting what people have accomplished and done by showing conversations with them, showing their accomplishments, and so forth. Television can do some fantastic things along these lines if we're willing to do it.

With respect to straight preaching: Unless it's very simple preaching, it's not going to be very effective on television. Usually the simpler the better. Here's where we get into the problems. How simple do you go? How much do you begin to throw out to get a message that will appeal to a mass audience and can be communicated through this technology? There are people out there who've dropped sin out of the picture. Sin complicates things too much. They want a very, very simple kind of message that everything will work out. Basically, Romans 8:28 without having to be a Christian. That becomes problematic.

Part of the problem is the cost of TV. This is not inherent in the technology, but there's a tremendous cost. If you're going to bring money in, you have to tell people by and large what they want to hear. If you're prophetic in a way that disturbs people, discomforts them, they're not necessarily going to be your supporters. So you're driven, on the one hand, by things inherent in the technology to simplify the message, and then by the economics of television to come up with a message that confirms what people either believe or want to believe—and here's the real danger. It's not just a simplification to get people in the church door. Now it's a corruption of the message, and the general direction of religious TV today is toward what I consider to be terrible distortions of the gospel, principally in the "health and wealth" gospel. I think that television let loose in a market system used by religions will tend to move in the direction of the "health and wealth" gospel, because that confirms some basic American myths.

Interviewer: As you pointed out in your book on televangelism, that also tends to bring in more financial support, doesn't it?

Schultze: It brings in the financial support because you're confirming what people want to believe: "Amen, brother, I'm gonna send you my bucks because that's what I want to happen to me too." I say in that book—and I've been criticized by people for doing this—that that's what led to the *700 Club* being organized around the theme of healing. Their own market research showed that's what people wanted. Well, when we get to the point where the church is in pure marketing—not to understand where people are so we can take the real gospel and reach them, but so we can design our message around what people want to hear for audience share and donation and all—then we're destroying the gospel.

I think there are two kinds of prophets. There is the kind of prophet who says, "Thus saith the Lord. You may not like it, but thus saith the Lord. I may not be popular, but thus saith the Lord." Then there's the other kind of prophet who gets his or her authority based on telling people what they want to hear rather than what they should hear. That's the false prophet.

Interviewer: What does the Christian preacher need to do to help prepare a congregation to deal with what is happening to them in terms of the impact television is making on their families and their daily lives?

Schultze: We have to see the broad context here. Most church-related time is leisure time—that's where it comes from. Whether it's going to church on Sunday morning or doing something on Wednesday evening at church, it comes out of leisure

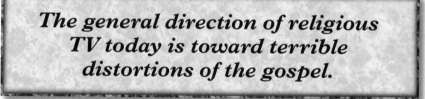

The general direction of religious TV today is toward terrible distortions of the gospel.

time. So I think the first thing that a pastor has to do is to convince the congregation that too much leisure time is spent doing things which are not productive—and not just productive in terms of specific religious goals, but in terms of family goals, in terms of all of the things that are really important about life. If we're seventy years old and look back on our lives and say what we wish we did more of—it's not going to be consuming more entertainment. That is far and away the single biggest thing that we do with our time.

I'm convinced that the place to start is to get people to reset their priorities with respect to leisure time—to encourage families to set limits on television viewing, film viewing, even radio listening, and so forth. And note: Set limits even on great stuff. People may have fantastic Christian videotapes that they just love, and they're edified by, and so forth, but when that takes up all their time without time put into relationships with family, relationship with church, evangelism, or whatever sort of things are the real needs in their community, I think it's selfishness. It's a kind of spiritual hedonism in a strange way. So that's number one and I think that can be done most effectively—here's the trick—not by being negative about what people are doing, but providing some positive alternatives—the kinds of activities that will promote warm loving relationships, what fellowship should really be. Given a choice, if they've experienced both, people in a congregation will pick the fellowship instead of picking the leisure entertainment stuff. If it's real fellowship, they will choose that every time, because it's where our real human needs are.

Let me give you an example. In my church we started a program called "Dinner for Eight," because small-group theory says when you get above eight people it's hard to have everybody involved. What we do is carve up the congregation into groups of eight with some couples, some singles, and so forth. Certain nights of the week we get together for dinner at people's homes. People bring different dishes, start out with dinner together, and then just talk about their lives. In our church, this has developed relationships among people who often were reluctant to shake someone's hand in church because they weren't sure of their name. It's mind-boggling that we could consider *that* the body of Christ—when you don't even know who this person is and you're there every Sunday with them.

We found that sports activities were a bait. We have three baseball teams in my church. We only have 120 families. We have three baseball teams; one of them is coed. We get together on a baseball field, play other teams, talk in the dugout, talk after the game, get there before the game to practice, and so forth. Someone said to me recently that they think more ministry is going on at those ball games and at "Dinner for Eight" than at our formal church programs. What have we done? We realized that formal church programs may not really help develop the kinds of interpersonal communication that will become the solid basis for church life that we need. So we decided to be very creative about what we use here so people want to come to church. If they know who these other people are, they want to talk with them at church. They want to do other things with them, so that's the place to start.

The next thing to do, which I think is really important, is to slowly bring in more of a cultural critique, and not just from the pulpit. One church in my area has started something very interesting. They have people agree in advance the Sunday before to see a certain film that week at a movie house. Now they're careful about what they select. They don't want the awful stuff. They see it that week, and on Sunday morning there is one class which is dedicated to people coming together and simply discussing that film. It may not be a film that's oriented toward adults. It may be the one that's most popular with their teenagers, and their teenagers don't want the parents to go with them to it because that embarrasses them. So they go out and see this film—*Wayne's World* or some other crazy thing—and they get together and talk about it. What does this say about our kids and where they're at and so forth? Try and grapple with this. I like the idea of churches taking spaces in their Sunday bulletins and having people make suggestions about TV programs, films, recordings, or whatever they found that they think has some redeeming value. These things may not be produced by Christians, but people may say, "Hey, I just saw this film, *Tender Mercies* or *Trip to Bountiful* or something else, and you know, I was amazed this was a Hollywood product." So the local body becomes a unit where together they start going out and consuming some of the same entertainment products; then they bring those within the discourse in the congregation. I think all of that is really helpful.

Preachers can't do it alone. What preachers can do is excite some other people to get things going in the congregation. It can't all be done from the pulpit. You can't put the burden for all of this on the preacher, but the preacher can be visionary and can take some risks that other people may not want to take in order to make some of these sorts of things happen.

Interviewer: I'm seeing an increasing use of Christian videotapes within the church for programming, from the children's church or the Sunday school class gathered around the tube watching the Bible story on video, to the whole congregation sitting around watching James Dobson, Tony Campolo, or some other good speaker on video. Obviously that brings some resources that would otherwise not be available. But are we sending some dangerous messages by using that medium in that way?

Schultze: First of all, video can be a very good medium for simple teaching, as I said before. With simple teaching, you can do some fantastic stuff with video. You can bring in some quality speakers, some quality material that it's hard to get locally. So there are some benefits there. That's the good side of it. The bad side of it is that churches are starting to become so dependent on this that they are disenfranchising their own laity from the responsibility of doing these things themselves. The pastors are more and more becoming sort of professionals who are responsible for everything, and the gifts of the laity are not being used adequately.

One of the things we decided in my church was to figure out how to use the gifts across the board in the congregation and promote this strongly—not just giving people work that they don't want to do, but trying to figure out what people's gifts are so that they get a sense of ownership. We have people who are experts in all kinds of things. We've got people who are experts in investment. We could get a bunch of great videotapes on investment as stewardship from a Christian perspective. There's a lot of good stuff out there. But if we've got people in our congregation who are willing to talk about this and do it—why not use them? So I think we go outside for established, professionalized kinds of tapes and all only when we can't do that stuff very well inside.

Also, when we use the professional stuff from the outside, it should always be assumed that it's supplemented with congregational discussion. If that's not there, I think a lot of the value is lost. If that means taking a fifty-minute tape and only doing twenty minutes of it one week and then spending twenty-five minutes in a Sunday school class discussing it—chopping it up that way—I still think we should do it, because then it becomes part of the congregational discussion and dialogue. Then the results of that can more easily be led into what the church is doing. So I'm grateful for what's going on in video. I'm not the Postman type to want to throw it out, but on the other hand, I want to say, "Let's be careful about how we use it—how we integrate it."

Interviewer: Do you have any final words of advice, caution, or encouragement to preachers relating to television, their use of television—how they should deal with it or adapt to it?

Schultze: The worst thing that a preacher can do is be defined by the congregation as someone who's negative about the media and not balanced about the media. Because then that sort of preacher will be tuned out. No matter what the adults in the congregation say, they've got certain media that they like. It's especially true with young people, so a preacher needs to convey both from the pulpit and interpersonal conversation a sense that media, like the creation overall, has a combination of the grace of God and the evidence for the fall in it, and so discernment is necessary. That's important—to get across that kind of credible position.

Another thing I would say is that a preacher should always be looking at ways of making use of local resources, within or outside the congregation, rather than assuming the preacher needs to deal with this problem completely alone. There are always resources around. There may be schools around with people who know something about this stuff, and so on. Look for those people, make use of them. The professionalization of the clergy has ended up in putting too much of the burden for all of this on just the preachers, and we need to figure out ways that we can enfranchise the laity in this.

July/August 1993

18

PREACHING TO JOE SECULAR

William L. Self

Though Atlanta is a city of churches, Wieuca Road Baptist Church is an enduring phenomenon. Once the magnet church for a generation of southern suburbanites, Wieuca Road is surrounded by bustling Buckhead, Atlanta's more intriguing urban landscape. It is a strange blending of southern mansions and urban canyons of reflective glass.

Wieuca Road stands as a symbol of ministry in the New South—and the New America. For over twenty years, William L. Self stood in the elegant pulpit at Wieuca Road, bridging the transition in the community as the minister to that several-thousand-member congregation. Today Self is preaching in the north Atlanta suburb of Alpharetta as pastor of the fast-growing Johns Creek Baptist Church.

One of the most popular pulpit communicators in America, Self is witty, incisive, and often controversial. He is never at a loss for words.

Interviewer: You have established a much-deserved reputation for effective preaching. How would you define biblical preaching?

Self: Biblical preaching is touching the needs of people with the message of the Bible—a message which is ultimately nothing other than Jesus Christ. That is biblical preaching. It starts with the need and comes back to the Bible, rather than starting with the Bible and going to the need.

I really don't think that the man in the pew—the secular man—is hungry to know what the Bible says. He is hungry for control of his life, hungry to get his life straightened out, hungry to "get his itches scratched." Biblical preaching is taking that point of need and leading the needy to the source of help—the Bible.

For most secular Americans—and it is to the secular mind that I target my preaching—the Bible is just another book. That is not what I believe about the Bible; it is a frank recognition that to the secular mind there may not be any great difference between the Bible, the Koran, Kahlil Gibran, or Rudyard Kipling. It falls to the preacher to demonstrate that it is the Bible which ultimately answers the great issues of life and meets the deepest human needs.

Interviewer: In recent years, preaching theorists have drawn attention to the assumptions underlying different models of biblical preaching by indicating where, in each model, the authority of the Word is basic. Is the Word located in the text, in the preaching event, or at the ear of the hearer? Is it not important to recognize the authority of the Word as primary in all three?

Self: Yes, the Word of God is found in all those places—the text, the sermon, and the ear. It is most ultimately in the biblical text. Biblical preaching is that mysterious arcing between the written text and the human need. It is a lively Word, an explosive Word, and it is a larger issue than we can fathom. We do not give this enough thought.

Interviewer: What are the basics of preaching to the secular mind? Where do you begin the process?

Self: I begin with the perceived need brought to the preaching event by the person in the pew. I don't really believe that the man in the pew comes with a burning personal need to know about the prodigal son. I don't think he or she has been awake at night worrying about what Paul meant by "work out your own salvation." I have never met a yuppie wrestling with the authorship of Hebrews. They just don't care about these issues. Most don't know these *are* issues.

The people I preach to range from the Atlanta street people to yuppies in their power ties and BMWs. The casual observer would not see much in common between these people, but their commonality is a sense of need. I begin there, address that need, and walk with them into a reservoir of meaning within the Bible. That will feed them at their point of greatest need.

Interviewer: What model of preaching do you find most effective? To what extent do you utilize propositional preaching, narrative models, and other preaching paradigms?

Self: I find that narrative preaching fits my understanding of how the biblical message will meet the human need. The great narratives of the Bible—from Samson to the prodigal son—represent deep rivers out of this reservoir of meaning.

I do not find myself doing much propositional preaching. There are congregations where propositional preaching is most appropriate—but that is not where I serve. The secular individual is not ready to balance out propositions unrelated to his or her perceived need.

Interviewer: How does the biblical text speak in this process?

Self: The text speaks after the individual's need and interest have been arrested. The text *speaks* at all levels, but our task as preachers is to identify the point at which it is best *heard*. It is heard when the text becomes the solution to the need.

Let me illustrate it this way: The secular individual comes to the pew with deep issues and needs at stake—though he may not really understand that at the time. He comes with a sense of worry or frustration, a basic lack of meaning in his life. She may come with a traumatic existential question: "Why did my fourteen-year-old daughter die last night in an accident?"

In the midst of this kind of basic question, the text speaks with authority. A text from Job, Paul, or the wisdom literature will speak to that grieving mother as no secular text can ever speak.

When this arcing takes place, you cannot confuse the biblical texts with the epigrams of an almanac or any other secular text.

It is not the preacher's responsibility to make that arc. All I can do is to bring the need to the text—get them juxtaposed—and trust the Holy Spirit and the presence of Christ to perform that mysterious arcing between our need and the gospel. It is just not possible for the preacher to accomplish this arcing.

I want to underscore this central point: I really *do* believe that Joe Secular does not see much difference between the Bible, an almanac, or Kahlil Gibran, unless that arcing takes place. You

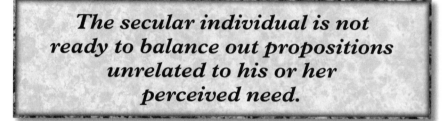

The secular individual is not ready to balance out propositions unrelated to his or her perceived need.

can see the secular mind pick up a folk song and make that their text—a secular text. We had a lot of that in the '60s and '70s. Even graffiti can become a text.

The fact that the biblical texts are found in a black book with gold edges does not impress the secular mind. What reaches even the most secular individuals, however, is when the Word of God authenticates itself in their life at the point of need. Then the authenticity is unmistakable.

Interviewer: How do you determine the needs of your hearers?

Self: You do a lot of listening. There are periods of time that I plunge into people like I would plunge into a swimming pool, walking among them. I spend a lot of time in the secular community. I may not spend enough time in the stained-glass community as I should. I invest my time in those events in the community which are not religious—civic clubs, professional meetings, business groups—and I do a lot of listening there. I get the pulse of where the people are. Just by listening and observing these groups, you get a sense of what those needs are.

You can also find the needs in the literature the secular mind is reading. Graham Greene speaks to those needs. Actually, most novelists speak to the secular mind and those needs. The religious community is often guilty of answering questions the secular mind isn't asking. If they do tackle some of these issues, they must do so in a way which will please the religious community.

Novelists like Graham Greene and John Updike may talk more about life than many of us are preaching. That is an indictment of the church. If we preach to the stained-glass ghetto, we must not suffer under the comfortable illusion that we are reaching the secular culture.

Interviewer: How has your preaching changed? You have been at Wieuca Road for over twenty years. How have the church and its community changed? You have said elsewhere that it is a different church from that of twenty years ago.

Self: That is so right. When I went to Wieuca Road, it was a burgeoning suburban church. As I look back on it, it was a cakewalk. Twenty years ago, people were moving into this community by the thousands. Atlanta was moving north—right in our direction. Anyone with his head screwed on straight could have built that church. But America changed. Wieuca Road changed.

Somewhere along the line, the suburban station wagon set moved on out, and we started finding the broken urban man in his sports car and second or third marriage. Our part of Atlanta is a different community. Yuppies, singles, street people, and midlife persons moved in—but many are not in the community for long. We had to deal with all this. My preaching has changed as I have focused on a different set of needs. Furthermore, I think I now have a better idea of how to address this.

I did go through a period when I bowed to Baal and tried to stay in the traditional models—three points and a poem. I would explain to the congregation the distance from Jerusalem to Jericho. In the last eight to ten years, I have discovered this other approach. I am more certain of it than ever, because I have seen it meet the real needs of real people.

Interviewer: How else has your preaching changed? Would those who have sat in those pews for the past twenty years discern the changes?

Self: I really think my preaching is better now, to be honest. I know it is more carefully targeted. I am more certain about what I am after when I step into the pulpit. I know where I am headed and what I hope will be accomplished. The entire service is more need oriented.

That does not mean that I do all life-situation preaching, but whatever style of sermon I preach, it must first ask the question: What are the listener's needs? I want to begin with the "hook" represented by his need.

As I prepare messages, I think of the guy in the pew. I keep a photograph of the church filled with people before me as I prepare. I look at that photograph and ask, "How does this fit John or Mary?" and so forth. Occasionally, I will sit by myself in the sanctuary, and through my imagination I listen to myself preach the sermon. As I do this, I ask myself, "Where is Joe Secular connecting with this?"

I also think my preaching is now more biblical. I think that the relationship between the biblical text and my sermon is more authentic now than it was twenty years ago. It is better researched.

Beyond that, I think the text and the message now "fit" better. A text is used because it speaks genuinely to the issue—and not because it sounds good to a religious audience.

Interviewer: What tangible suggestions would you offer to your fellow preachers? Speak to the thousands of preachers who must, in Fred Craddock's words, "get up a sermon every Sunday."

Self: I have just converted to something every veteran preacher knows. I am a late convert here—I did it kicking and screaming—but it has given the biggest release I have ever had. I now plan a year's pulpit work ahead, or at least nine months ahead. I really don't plan the three summer months.

I go away into the mountains and force myself to do it, to plan those nine months of preaching. After the agony comes the release. It is really the most relaxing experience of my life. There is now a sense of wholeness about my preaching ministry—in contrast to the shotgun approach of my earlier ministry. I grieve over the wasted years when I did not do this.

Interviewer: What about your reading? What do you find yourself reading as you think about the secular mind and the task of preaching?

Self: That is my other tangible suggestion: Read as widely as you possibly can. Subscribe to magazines and journals most folks wouldn't read. Get the *New York Times* and read the book review section and the magazine section. Take a Sabbath to read. No one has any more time than anyone else. We all suffer under the same time pressure. Take a short Sabbath every week to read. Let it percolate in your head until you can focus it out, then preach it out. To paraphrase Karl Barth, take the Bible in one hand and the newspaper in the other. You must bridge the two.

Interviewer: You have the opportunity in these pages to speak to several thousand preaching colleagues. What is the one thing you would want to say to them?

Self: Preaching is worth the effort. It is the greatest thing in the world if you are called to do it. It is a divine madness, but, speaking as one who has done it all his life, I would do it all again. I would *pay* for this privilege.

Furthermore, the church is worth it—it really is. Don't despair over the church or give up on it. Every preacher is tempted to do that at one time or another. But the church is where the action is. If God is going to do anything in this world, he is going to do it through his church.

November/December 1988

THEOLOGY AND PREACHING TODAY

R. C. Sproul

R. C. Sproul has built an international ministry of writing and teaching through Ligonier Ministries, based in Orlando, Florida. A graduate of Westminster College, Pittsburgh Theological Seminary, and the Free University of Amsterdam, Sproul also serves as professor at Knox Theological Seminary in Fort Lauderdale. He is an author of many books and a frequent preacher in pulpits across America.

Interviewer: One of your books is entitled *Doubt and Assurance.* In our own day, doubt is one of the most pervasive senses that people have in this culture. How do you describe the work of the preacher in helping people deal with issues of doubt and providing assurance?

Sproul: You may remember the Congress on the Bible that was held several years ago in San Diego. I had been asked to give the wrap-up message that night, and I spoke on the assurance of salvation. I did that because I had come to the conviction that the single most important issue in strengthening the Christian's personal spiritual growth, development, and sanctification is his assurance of salvation. The Bible commands us to make our calling and election assured—we are not to be wavering and tossed to and fro.

Over the years, I've thought a lot about that—personally, existentially, and theologically. Unless I get that settled in my life as a Christian, that I am truly in a state of grace, I am open to every kind of paralysis that can afflict me. I have spent most of my ministry teaching not only theology, but also apologetics. As a Reformed theologian, the question I get all the time is, "If you believe that election is something that's established from the foundation of the world, why would you even bother with apologetics? Why waste any time on it? If a person is elect, they're going to come to faith, and if they're not, they're not. So why should you be out there arguing for the truth of the Christian faith?"

The value of apologetics goes way beyond evangelism. It's a real ministry to the Christian, because the Christian lives his or her whole life echoing the apostolic words, "I believe Lord; help thou mine unbelief." Our faith is never without the dross mixed in, and it's never pure. We are assailed by doubts from all different areas, and it's a daily thing.

So when the people gather in church on Sunday morning, their confidence level of faith is on a sliding scale, vacillating up and down. One of the key responsibilities of preaching is to strengthen faith, to encourage the believer, to bring them afresh before the Word of God and the comforting assurance that comes with the presence of the Spirit in the Word. So I think ministering to people's doubts in preaching is a very important element.

Interviewer: How do you see a pastor weaving apologetics into the total preaching ministry? Every spring, many pastors will preach Easter sermons offering evidences for the resurrection. That is certainly a use of apologetics in the pulpit, but how do you move beyond that?

Sproul: I don't know that there's one "canned" technique that can be used here, but I can look at a couple of models in church history that I find helpful. Let me begin with a negative model. You mentioned the Easter experience. We sing a hymn: "He lives! He lives! Christ Jesus lives today. He walks with me . . . You ask me how I know he lives? He lives within my heart." Well, if that's the only reason I know he lives, I don't have any knowledge whatsoever, because the basic affirmation of the Easter message is that Christ lives apart from "within my heart"—he lives outside my heart. He really is alive. It's not just the subjective feeling that makes my heart flutter now and then. It's the reality. That reality, before it can ever move and stir the heart, first of all has to be grasped to some degree by the mind. So now we have the role of apologetics.

Look at two models from two great preachers. I would consider Jonathan Edwards the greatest preacher this nation has ever produced. Edwards had a standard pattern to his sermons; he would do basically three things in each of his sermons. The first part of his sermon was vigorous and thorough exposition and exegesis of the text from which he was preaching. That's the central thrust of his preaching—the text. But then he would always have a section on what we would call natural reason, which was corroborative for Edwards.

For example, when he wrote his masterpiece on original sin, he went through an exposition of the biblical texts that teach original sin. Then when he was done with that, he said, "Let's suppose there was no Bible. How could we account for the universality of evil in the world? Nature itself reveals that there had to have been some kind of fall because sin is universal." He would then give arguments from reason showing that he was not just appealing to a specific religious authority.

The third segment of his sermons was always practical application in which he would drive home the truth that he had just been developing. That's Edwards, and he's usually considered out-of-date, archaic, antiquated, and so on. Maybe that's why great awakenings are antiquated.

The other great preacher whom I see who wove apologetics frequently into his preaching was Paul of Tarsus. His preaching began principally in the marketplace, where he debated and dialogued every day, proclaiming Christianity. In the midst of it, he would be giving the reasons why he believed. He would quote the Scriptures, as he did before Agrippa. He was preaching there when he was giving his defense; he appealed to the prophets before Agrippa, then he appealed to his own eyewitness experience. First Corinthians 15 is a masterpiece of the combination

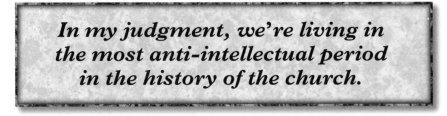

In my judgment, we're living in the most anti-intellectual period in the history of the church.

of an appeal to the Bible and an appeal to a logically reasoned case for the position Paul was describing. In this day and age, we've become schizophrenic; logic is something that the devil does, something that the unbeliever leans on, as if it's unspiritual to think or reason. This is an anti-apologetic age. I live it every day.

Interviewer: Though many of the people in Edwards's congregation may have been unconverted, there was within that culture a basic acceptance of at least the validity of Scripture. There was an appreciation, an honor, and a respect for Scripture. That is increasingly no longer present in American life.

Sproul: We can't assume there's a basic acceptance, that's right.

Interviewer: How does that affect the particular approach that one takes in preaching, not simply in approaching the text, but perhaps in the use of natural reason? Based on the kind of cultural setting in which we're now working, how would you update Edwards's approach?

Sproul: What I have done, and what I would recommend is to look at the cultural situation in which we find ourselves. I recognize that it's passé to appeal to reason, and it's also passé to appeal to the authority of the Bible. The image of Billy Graham standing up and saying, "The Bible says . . . the Bible says . . . the Bible says," is considered useless in this day and age. Preachers are looking acutely at the current trends in culture and trying to adjust our techniques and methods of communication to that culture in ways relevant to the modern situation.

In my judgment, we're living in the most anti-intellectual period in the history of the church. I don't mean antiscience; I don't mean antitechnology; I mean anti-mind. Preachers and others don't want to engage the mind. We're almost pathologically programming people to this anti-intellectual method through the use of television and other impressionistic media. Many spokesmen are saying you have to adjust to that situation, and that the worst approach to people today is a rational appeal or even a pure exegetical admonition from Scripture.

I'm going to be bold enough to say straight out, "Hey, I'm old enough, I'm ready to die, I don't care about my reputation!" People respond to my preaching, and I break every rule I've just mentioned. I'll tell you why I do it. I don't care what the culture is like. I know two things—that God made us with minds, and that he made the mind as the chief organ of receiving information, analyzing that information, and responding to it. To accommodate our preaching to a temporary fad of mindlessness is to deny the very nature of divine creation.

If there's any secret to preaching today, I think it would be that the preacher who will appeal to the mind is the one who is going to get a much greater and broader hearing than the one who seeks to play catch-up with this crazy cultural direction. Cultural trends and attitudes and views of the Bible vacillate enormously, but the power of the Word of God hasn't changed—it's transcendent—and the preacher who preaches that faithfully, consistently, and boldly sees incredible results from such preaching.

People's basic makeup does not change—their biases change, their tastes change—but their constituent makeup doesn't change from culture to culture or from generation to generation, and the Word of God doesn't change either. That's where I am.

Interviewer: The power in the Word inherently transcends whatever the cultural situation may be?

Sproul: What I'm saying is that if Jonathan Edwards walked into a church today and preached, in three years they'd have a megachurch, and everybody would wonder why we quit preaching like Edwards in the first place!

Interviewer: Do you believe that some of the contemporary trends in worship are actually feeding that kind of mindlessness? What do you think of some of the more current worship styles?

Sproul: I have ambivalent feelings—but the deepest feeling I can isolate is grief. When I say I have ambivalent feelings, on the one side I'm excited that there are people courageous enough to challenge traditions that have been accepted uncritically, people who are obviously motivated to find ways to communicate the gospel to our contemporary society, and are willing to challenge traditions that may be barriers to expressing that.

When I look at the motives for that, as I discern them in people I talk to who are on the cutting edge of these new techniques and so on, I'm excited by their creativity and by their passion. When I see some of the directions in which it is going, however, that's the other side of the ambivalence.

Phrases like "seeker-sensitive worship" scare me to death. In the first place, being Reformed in my understanding of the Bible, I don't believe people seek after God until after they're converted. The Bible I read tells me that no one seeks after God— no one—and that seeking God is the business of the Christian. And so this idea that there are people out there searching for God—as though God is hiding and they can't find him—is as foreign to the Bible as I can imagine. I agree with Thomas Aquinas that people outside of Christ are definitely seeking something. They're seeking happiness, they're seeking peace of mind, they're seeking relief from guilt, they're seeking meaning to their lives—all of that. They're seeking for the benefits that only God can give them; but they're not seeking for God, they're running from God. No, I'm not interested in accommodating worship to the unbeliever.

There is one period of time during the week when the family of God, the people of God, the body of Christ is to come together to be nurtured and fed as believers. That experience of worship is absolutely vital to the Christian life, and in a very real sense, it's not for the unbeliever. The unbeliever is a spectator to that. Don't misunderstand what I'm saying—I love the aggressive emphasis on evangelism, but don't bring it into the worship service, because to encourage an unbeliever to participate in worship is to encourage him to be involved in blasphemy, because it's not honest worship. It's not worship in spirit and in truth.

As for the techniques that are used to bring them in—I had an astute theological observer say to me that the new move toward liberalism and unbelief will not come through defections in theology, but it will be carried by methodology, by this burning desire to be relevant.

It's easy to stand there and say, "I don't like that." Still, we have seen the failure of the traditional format to hold people in the life of the church. I'm involved in a little church in Orlando where we are committed to a more classical, liturgical form of worship, and I realize how that can become endless repetition—meaningless repetition, vacuous, empty formalism. Yet when that ritual is informed by clear preaching of the content and its meaning and the people become alert to it, it can be so, so rich. What I hear is that people are expressing a hunger and a wistful sense about the lack of a meaningful experience of worship.

Preaching is not to be the center of Sunday morning worship. As much as I'm committed to preaching, when God developed a tabernacle and a temple, it was first called the house of prayer. Preaching and teaching are things that took place in the synagogue. We saw what happened in the development of the Roman church when the liturgy became vacuous and obscured the message of the gospel. With the Reformation, we wanted to restore the Word to the center of the Christian life—and I think it should be the center of the Christian life—but now preaching is in danger of eclipsing worship.

So you have one group trying to make worship more relevant by finding contemporary modes and means, while other people are looking to the past to find a rich liturgy. They're both searching for the same thing. They're searching for a meaningful worship experience. We have to be reawakened to a sense of the presence of God and the majesty of God. Unless we have that sense of the presence of God, there's nothing for the soul to relate to.

Interviewer: Tell me about your own approach to preaching.

Sproul: When I was a young man, I wrote out all my sermons and memorized them. Then I came under the influence of Robert J. Lamont, the former pastor of the First Presbyterian

Church of Pittsburgh. Lamont talked to me about extemporaneous preaching. It was a fateful day in my life because it was the day my digestive system was destroyed.

Lamont told me that he preached without notes, but what he meant by spontaneous preaching was not "winging it." He immersed himself in the text, studied all the commentaries, thought about the text from every different angle, existentially got involved in the text. In other words, he tried to put himself in the life situation from which the text came—let that text get into his mind and then into his bloodstream. He would think about it during the week, and think about concrete life illustrations that would communicate the basic message he was trying to give. He would think in terms of his opening and where he was trying to go, select a couple of key illustrations, and that was it. Then he went into the pulpit trusting his mind and his ability to articulate and to get into a kind of a zone of communication with his people.

We do this all the time when we're talking with each other. We don't have notes in front of us. We call upon our normal vocabulary patterns and our minds to think ahead of our mouths. He encouraged me to preach like that—and it was terrifying! That's what I did.

I speak anywhere from three hundred to five hundred times a year. I sometimes think of how dreadful it would be if I had to write every one of them down. But not having a manuscript—not even a printed outline—evokes in me all kinds of anxiety. That's what I meant when I said Lamont's advice to me literally destroyed my digestive system. I don't think I've properly digested a meal in thirty years because of losing the security of having that manuscript.

Teaching has been an enormous help, because teaching theology in the classroom for thirty years has provided a reservoir of content and concepts to draw from when I'm dealing with texts.

Interviewer: I find more and more preachers are avoiding notes altogether. And for those who do it well, it improves communication.

Sproul: Notes are a terrible barrier to communication. I had a pastor come to me and say, "I would really like for you to help me with my preaching by critiquing it." The Sunday afterwards, while listening to him preach from a full manuscript, I performed a simple exercise: Every time he broke eye contact with us, I made a mark on a paper. We met afterwards and he asked, "Well, what about it?" I replied, "Let me ask you a question. How many times in your twenty-two-minute sermon did you break eye contact with the congregation and look at your manuscript?" He said, "Well, maybe eighteen times." Then I turned the paper over and showed him the marks—162 times. He just about died! I continued, "Just as soon as you would start to communicate to us, you would interrupt the communication by looking down. Just once, preach without that manuscript. You'll forget some things you wanted to remember; there are some trade-offs here, obviously. You'll have less confidence. But I want you to try it just once," I advised.

Well, he was terrified—but he did without his manuscript. The first time he did, the people didn't realize why they sensed a difference, but there was a quantum leap in communication. The response of the congregation overwhelmed him. Now he never uses a manuscript. I've seen this happen again and again and again—but a price is paid for it.

Interviewer: If you had just one or two messages for preachers who are struggling to communicate the gospel in this age, what would you share with them?

Sproul: Two things. One, focus your preaching on the character of God. Two, preach at least 75 percent of your sermons from the Old Testament, for three reasons: First, the Old Testament's primary achievement is revealing the character of God—God the Father; second, the Old Testament gives you the most incredible narratives (I'm big on preaching from narratives because people will listen ten times as hard to a story as they will to an abstract lesson); and third, the Old Testament provides a scenario of interaction between God and real people, and it's eminently contemporary. There's just a wealth of application in that arena.

March/April 1994

CREATING THE BRIDGE

John R. W. Stott

John R. W. Stott has emerged in the last half of the twentieth century as one of the leading evangelical preachers in the world. His ministry has spanned decades and continents, combining his missionary zeal with the timeless message of the gospel.

For many years the rector of All Souls' Church in London, Stott is also the founder and director of the London Institute for Contemporary Christianity. His preaching ministry stands as a model of the effective communication of biblical truth to secular men and women.

The author of several worthy books, Stott is perhaps best known in the United States through his involvement with the URBANA mission conferences. His voice and pen have been among the most determinative forces in the development of the contemporary evangelical movement in the Church of England and throughout the world.

Interviewer: You have staked your ministry on biblical preaching and have established a worldwide reputation for the effective communication of the gospel. How do you define biblical preaching?

Stott: I believe that to preach or to expound the Scripture is to open up the inspired text with such faithfulness and sensitivity that God's voice is heard and his people obey him. I gave that definition at the Congress on Biblical Exposition and I stand by it, but let me expand a moment.

My definition deliberately includes several implications concerning the Scripture. First, it is a uniquely inspired text. Second, the Scripture must be opened up. It comes to us partially closed, with problems which must be opened up. Beyond this, we must expound it with faithfulness and sensitivity. Faithfulness relates to the Scripture itself. Sensitivity relates to the modern world. The preacher must give careful attention to both.

We must always be faithful to the text, and yet ever sensitive to the modern world and its concerns and needs. When this happens, the preacher can come with two expectations: First, that God's voice will be heard, because he speaks through what he has spoken in the Bible. Second, that God's people will obey him—that they will respond to his Word as it is preached.

Interviewer: You obviously have a very high regard for preaching. In *Between Two Worlds,* you wrote extensively of the glory of preaching, even going so far as to suggest that "preaching is indispensable to Christianity."

We are now coming out of an era in which preaching was thought less and less relevant to the church and its world. Even in those days, you were outspoken in your affirmation of the preaching event and its centrality. Has your mind changed?

Stott: To the contrary! I still believe that preaching is the key to the renewal of the church. I am an impenitent believer in the power of preaching. I know all the arguments against it—that the television age has rendered preaching useless, that we are a spectator generation, that people are bored with the spoken word, disenchanted with any communication by spoken words alone. All these things are said these days.

Nevertheless, when a man of God stands before the people of God with the Word of God in his hand and the Spirit of God in his heart, you have a unique opportunity for communication. I fully agree with Martyn Lloyd-Jones that the decadent periods in the history of the church have always been those periods marked by preaching in decline. That is a negative statement. The positive counterpart is that churches grow to maturity when the Word of God is faithfully and sensitively expounded to them.

If it is true that a human being cannot live by bread only, but by every word which proceeds out of the mouth of God, then it also is true of churches. Churches live, grow, and thrive in response to the Word of God. I have seen congregations come alive by the faithful and systematic unfolding of the Word of God.

Interviewer: You have pictured the great challenge of preaching as creating a bridge between two worlds—the world of the biblical text and the world of the contemporary hearer. That chasm seems ever more imposing in the modern world. How can the preacher really bridge that chasm?

Stott: Any bridge, if it is to be effective, must be firmly grounded on both sides of the canyon. To build a bridge between the modern world and the biblical world, we must first be careful students of both. We must be ever engaged in careful biblical exegesis, conscientiously and continually, and yet also involved in careful study of the contemporary context. Only this will allow us to relate one to the other.

I find it helpful in my own study to ask two questions of the text—and in the right order. First, "What does it mean?" and second, "What does it say?" The answer to the first is determined by the original author. I am fond of citing E. D. Hirsch in his book *Validity in Interpretation,* when he wrote, "The text means what its author meant." That is my major quarrel with the existentialists, who say that the text means what it means to me—the reader—independent of what the author meant. We must say "no" to that. A text means primarily what its author meant. It is the author who establishes the meaning of the text.

Beyond that, we must accept the discipline of grammatical and historical exegesis, of thinking ourselves back into the historical, geographical, cultural, and social situation in which the author was writing. We must do this to understand what the text means. It cannot be neglected.

The second question moves us from the original meaning of the text to its contemporary message, "What does it say?" If we ask the first question without asking the second, we lapse into antiquarianism, unrelated to modern reality.

On the other hand, if we leap to the second question—"What does it say today?"—we lapse into existentialism, unrelated to the reality of biblical revelation. We have to relate the past revelation of God to the present reality of the modern world.

Interviewer: That requires a double exegesis—an exegesis of the text and also an exegesis of life. Is it your opinion that most evangelicals are better exegetes of the text than they are of life?

Stott: Oh, I am sure of it. I am myself and always have been a better student of Scripture than of the present reality. We love the Bible, read it, and study it, and all our preaching comes out of the Bible. Very often it does not land on the other side of that chasm. It is never earthed in reality.

The attractiveness of liberal or radical preaching, whatever it is called these days, is that it tends to be done by genuinely modern people who live in the modern world, understand it, and

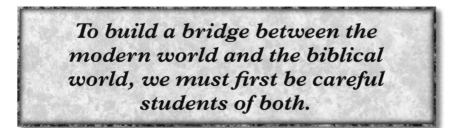

To build a bridge between the modern world and the biblical world, we must first be careful students of both.

relate to it. But their message often does not come from the Bible. Their message is never rooted in the textual side of the chasm. We must combine the two relevant questions.

Interviewer: Most of us think of ourselves as modern persons, and yet we may lack a suitable hermeneutic of the contemporary. What have you found to be helpful as you seek to be a better student of the contemporary world?

Stott: I mentioned in *Between Two Worlds* how very helpful I found involvement in a reading group I founded about fifteen years ago. They are graduates and professional people—doctors,

an architect, an attorney, teachers, and so on. All are committed to Christ and the Scripture and yet anxious to be modern
and contemporary people. We meet every month or so when I
am in London.

We decide to read a particular book, or see a particular play
or exhibition, and spend the evening discussing it. We give most
attention to books. We go around the circle and give our immediate impression before eventually turning and asking, "Now,
what has the gospel to say to this?" I have found it enormously
helpful to be forced to think biblically about modern issues.

Interviewer: So you would point biblical preachers not only
to the biblical text, but to a very wide reading?

Stott: Absolutely. I think wide reading is essential. We need
to listen to modern men and women and read what they are writing. We need to go to the movies, to watch television, to go to
the theater. The modern screen and stage are mirrors of the modern world. I seldom go on my own. I go with friends committed
to the same kind of careful understanding.

Interviewer: You have made it clear that you see preaching
as a glorious calling and vocation. What do you see as the greatest contemporary need in preaching? Where is biblical preaching falling tragically short?

Stott: Well, in the more liberal churches, it falls woefully short
of being fully biblical. Among the evangelical churches, it falls
short by being less than fully contemporary. I can only repeat
the great need of struggling to understand the issues of the modern world. Nevertheless, there is a tremendous correlation
between the issues of the biblical world and the modern world.

People are actively seeking the very answers Jesus provides.
People are asking the very questions Jesus can answer, if only we
understand the questions the world is asking.

Interviewer: Your service over many years at All Souls'
Church in London had a tremendous impact throughout much
of the world. There, in the midst of London's busiest retail area,
you presented the gospel with great effectiveness and power. Did
your preaching change at all during your ministry at All Souls'?

Stott: I began with a very strong commitment to Scripture, a
very high view of its authority and inspiration. I have always loved

the Word of God—ever since I was converted. Therefore, I have always sought to exercise an expository or exegetical ministry.

In my early days, I used to think that my business was to expound and exegete the text; I am afraid I left the application to the Holy Spirit. It is amazing how you can conceal your laziness with a little pious phraseology! The Holy Spirit certainly can and does apply the Word for the people. But it is wrong to

> *People are asking the very questions Jesus can answer, if only we understand the questions the world is asking.*

deny our own responsibility in the application of the Word. All great preachers understand this. They focus on the conclusion, on the application of the text. This is what the Puritans called "preaching through to the heart." This is how my own preaching has changed. I have learned to add application to exposition—and this is the bridge-building across the chasm.

Interviewer: You have recently published a major volume on the cross—*The Cross of Christ*. This has always been central to your preaching—and to all genuinely Christian preaching. Do you perceive an inadequate focus on the cross in the pulpit today?

Stott: Indeed, so far as I can see, it is inadequate. I think we need to get back to the fact that the cross is the center of biblical Christianity. We must not allow those on the one hand to put the incarnation as primary, nor can we allow those on the other hand to put the primary focus on the resurrection.

Of course, the cross, the incarnation, and the resurrection belong together. There could have been no atonement without the incarnation or without the resurrection. The incarnation prepares for the atonement and the resurrection endorses the atonement, so they always belong together.

Yet the New Testament is very clear that the cross stands at the center. It worries me that some evangelicals do not focus on

Christ crucified as the center. Of course, we preach the whole of biblical religion, but with the cross as central.

One of the surprises which came as a product of the research for the book was the discovery that most books on the cross focus only on the atonement. There is much the New Testament has to say about the cross which is not focused on the atonement. We are told, for example, to take up our cross and follow Christ. Communion is a cross-centered festival. There is the whole question of balance in the modern world. The problems of suffering and self-image are addressed by the cross. These issues appear quite differently when our worldview is dominated by the cross.

Interviewer: You are probably as well known in America as in England. Furthermore, you know America—its churches and its preachers. What would be your word to the servants of the Word on this side of the Atlantic?

Stott: I think my main word to American preachers is, as Stephen Olford has often said, that we belong in a study, not in an office. The symbol of our ministry is a Bible—not a telephone. We are ministers of the Word, not administrators, and we need to relearn the question of priority in every generation.

The apostles were in danger of being diverted from the ministry to which they had been called by Jesus—the ministry of Word and prayer. They were almost diverted into a social ministry for squabbling widows.

Now both are important, and both are ministries, but the apostles had been called to the ministry of the Word, not the ministry of tables. They had to delegate the ministry of the tables to other servants. We are not apostles, but there is the work of teaching that has come to us in the unfolding of the apostolic message of the New Testament. This is our priority as pastors and preachers.

Jesus preached to the crowds, to the group, and to the individual. He had the masses, the disciples, and individuals coming to him. He preached to crowds, taught the disciples, and counseled individuals. We must also have this focus. It is all in the ministry of the Word.

March/April 1989

PREACHING
AND THE HOLY SPIRIT

Chuck Swindoll

With a winsome smile, a contagious chuckle, and practical insights for Christian living, Chuck Swindoll has carved out a place as one of America's favorite preachers. Former pastor of the First Evangelical Free Church in Fullerton, California, and president of Dallas Theological Seminary, Swindoll is best known for his string of best-selling Christian books and for his popular radio ministry, *Insights for Living.* His book *Flying Closer to the Flame* prompted this discussion about the relationship of the Holy Spirit and the preaching task.

Interviewer: Your most recent book deals with the work of the Holy Spirit. How do you understand the relationship of the Spirit's work to the ministry of preaching?
Swindoll: I think that the Spirit of God is doing many things he never gets credit for. To start with, I think he prompts ideas and prepares the soil of our souls for certain subjects. I felt that

was true—definitely true—in my series on grace that led to *The Grace Awakening.* There were some things that we'd gone through that created some growing feelings—churnings within. We all have what I call a "churning place." That's not an original thought with me, but I have used those words which I got from another. I think the Spirit churns us—he prompts us—and in that process, I believe he begins to build the steam in our areas of motivation and instill a growing sense of passion. That's a word I've learned to really appreciate. In fact the subtitle for the book I'm doing is *A Passion for the Holy Spirit.*

I think in this growing sense of passion, we get direction for how we want to build a series of sermons. I haven't always thought through every message before I get going on it. So a series kind of shapes itself as I'm going along, like some novelists talk about doing a book. I begin with several things in mind I want to do, but often it takes a new direction in the middle of the series.

For that reason, I don't really do a full preaching calendar. Some people go on their vacations, or take six weeks off, and while they're away, they do this shaping of the next year. I used to do that, only to have it changed by the third or fourth week I was back. I thought, "Well, I don't need to do that again." It took me a couple of years to say, "I'm not going to spend all that time if it's going to be changing anyway." However, I do believe in planning and thinking things through, and I think that's where the Spirit of God is at work.

And then, of course, in the actual putting together of the message, I will look back sometimes and I will say that only the Spirit of God could have directed me. I don't know at the time that I'm aware of his working, but in the process of shaping my thoughts—when words flow, ideas keep on track, it's a wonderful thing to have that happen—I'm able to look back at the end of the week and think, "Why, it's obviously the work of the Spirit." I do morning and evening services, and how they tie in is again an amazing tapestry, the weaving of thoughts together. So I think the Spirit of God is engaged in that.

Then there is the actual delivery. There are times—I don't want this to sound spooky—but there are times I feel almost outside myself. You have that experience where you say (and even at the time you're delivering it you're thinking), "I could not have arranged these thoughts this well." I use notes when I preach, and so I will look down on occasion and I'll be three pages ahead of my notes—caught up in the movement of the message. And I think the Spirit of God is doing that.

Interviewer: That was once known as the "unction" of the Spirit. Today we identify it as the "anointing" of the Holy Spirit. How do you describe the experience?

Swindoll: What is the anointing of the Spirit? I don't think we can nail it down. It's broad; it transcends dimensions. I think his prompting, his motivational work, his allowing you to grow in passion—I think all of that falls under the umbrella of his anointing. So that when you've finished—and I really mean this sincerely—you feel like you don't deserve credit for it. You didn't do it. Sure, you used your voice box and you used your gestures, and maybe the words as you pull this thing to a conclusion, but in many ways he fueled the fire that set the thing off, and you look back and say, "Thank you."

I've driven home many a time thinking, "Thank you, Lord, for doing that." It sounds terribly simplistic, but I really mean it. I don't mean to say I sit down on Sunday morning and quickly put thoughts together. I've been working on it maybe two, three, four weeks. But in the actual delivery it's like, "My, how wonderful of the Spirit of God to do that for me."

Interviewer: Do you think as your ministry has matured— as you've grown older and more experienced—that you have a greater sense of the presence or the work of the Holy Spirit in your life?

Swindoll: No doubt, no doubt. I think early on, when we preachers are getting underway, we're a little overly concerned about those things that aren't that essential. As you get older, I think you realize there is really no one to fear but God himself. I asked Loren Sandy of the Navigators when he turned sixty, "What's the difference?" He had a wonderful answer: "I'm not afraid of anyone, but I'm more than ever afraid of God, fearful of this awesome God I serve." Age brings an awareness of the presence of God, the dependence upon him—not just for every heartbeat and every breath in your lungs, but for the shaping of a ministry. I've used that word several times already, but I really believe it takes the shape that's brought on by his presence. I think he warns us, I think he moves us in another direction.

At the same time, you've got to be right in your heart. I think it is Clarence McCartney who talks about sin in the life of the pastor in his book *Preaching without Notes.* He says when there

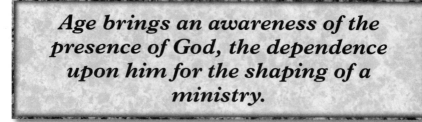

Age brings an awareness of the presence of God, the dependence upon him for the shaping of a ministry.

is a wrong in one's life, it haunts you all the way up the pulpit stairs. When there's purity, there's a freedom where you can step into the pulpit and you're freed from the filth of the flesh. So I think that sense of the awareness of God's presence is all from the Spirit.

Interviewer: The anointing of the Spirit in the life of the preacher is a difficult thing to describe.

Swindoll: It is. It's not like a ruler, exactly twelve inches long. This makes half the ruler and this makes the other half—it's just not like that. And I've got to tell you, too, there are times when there is a barrenness of soul where it is like pickaxing your way through granite, and you wonder, "Where is the Lord in this?" This book I wrote on the Holy Spirit is the hardest thing I've ever written. I can't really figure out why, because I loved the study that led to it. I loved the way the chapters were beginning to fall together, but putting those words down so that they were fair and yet interesting—here again I had a hard time. So I worked over titles of chapters and the way the chapters flowed together. I would take a half a chapter and throw it away—and I don't usually do that—and I'd start all over. Sometimes I'd stare at a blank page for two hours, and I rarely, if ever, in my life have done that. But this book seemed not to want to be written.

Interviewer: Did this book come out of a series of sermons?

Swindoll: I was in a series called "The Intimate Spirit." That was my series title. And out of the blue in a conversation with Byron Williamson, my friend at Word, he said, "We're thinking about your doing something on the Holy Spirit." I said, "Isn't that interesting. I'm doing something on the intimate Spirit." He said, "Tell me about that." Then he began to tell me, "You know, that's too good. Write me." In fact, I quoted part of his letter in my fifth or sixth message—and in the fifth or sixth chapter, which I call, "Draw Me Nearer, Nearer." That's where we got the idea of *Flying Closer to the Flame.* So yes, it grew out of a series, but the series was under way before I thought about a book, and I like that.

I didn't approach it from the perspective, "I need to do a book. Why don't I preach a series." I don't believe I've ever done that. In fact, the whole idea of the book *Grace Awakening* came from a series I did on "Amazing Grace." *Simple Faith* was another book—I did a series on the Sermon on the Mount which grew into that book. This is a helpful way to do it, because you've done a lot of your tool work. Once again, I think the Spirit of God is involved in that.

There's a great, intriguing section in 1 Corinthians 2:11 about the Spirit of God: "No man knows the thoughts of a man, but the spirit of man which is within him; even so, no one knows the thoughts of God but the Spirit of God." And the analogy is great. You know thoughts that you're having right now that I can't possibly know. Even if I sat with you for a week, I couldn't know the thoughts. So the Spirit of God knows the thoughts of God, and is able to delve in the depths of God. And I think we get our best thoughts when the Spirit of God dips into the well of the mind of God, brings it up like a bucket, pours it upon us, and we get some of those thoughts. They are so magnificent, and for us life-changing. As we communicate them, they become life-changing living water for other people who are thirsty. That sounds terribly pious, but I really believe that's the way it works!

Interviewer: It may be pious, but it's also biblical.

Swindoll: I think so too. And I like it that I can't specify it any more than that, so that I find myself surprised. I'm surprised at what I see. I was working on my messages for next Sunday—aren't we always! "Sunday's always three days away" we say on our staff. I got insights into a passage of Scripture out of Luke 12 that were terrific. I've never seen those things before; isn't that amazing? I think that's the Spirit's work.

I've said to Cynthia many times, "If I ever lose this, I'm finished." If I'm ever to the place where I don't get those fresh thoughts, I've got to hang it up.

Interviewer: And you can't teach that in a classroom.

Swindoll: You can't, that's what amazes me. The guys who are teaching on preaching—I don't know how they do it. I don't know how I'd get a set of notes together. In fact, I did some teaching for Trinity Seminary on their D.Min. program—there's an extension work going on out on the West Coast, and I taught on preaching two separate times. And in the midst of it I said, "You know what, folks? When it's all said and done, if the Spirit doesn't ignite this, it's no more than water in your gas tank—it's just liquid and it won't burn. But when he ignites it, it becomes fuel."

I'm reminded of the words of Amy Carmichael when she concludes that poem and she talks about, "Help me not to be a clod, make me thy fuel, flame of God." In fact, I could have quoted her in my book. I've just come to think of it, but that's it—"Make me thy fuel, flame of God." And when he does, I think everybody stands in awe—not of the preacher, but of the spoken, delivered Word that came from the mountain.

Interviewer: You can do all the study, all the spade work, and do the best preparation, but unless the Spirit anoints it . . .

Swindoll: It is what I call flatland—there's no scenery, no change in temperature, no color. There's no snow or seasons, no sunshine or rain. It's flatland. You're just driving over flatland, and we've all done that. The longest hour of my life—the longest week of my life—is the message that is being delivered. It's not that you're doing it in the flesh, it's just that for some reason the Spirit of God is lifted from it. Boy, I wish I knew those times. I'd sure take my vacation then. I'd stay away!

Interviewer: I think every pastor has had those times when it's just a dry season. What do you do in those dry seasons?

Swindoll: One thing is I remind myself I'm still called. I'm still God's man for this. It's not necessarily the time for me to be moving on somewhere else, because I'll take that with me. That's one warning I would say as I speak of my calling. I go back and I say, "I remember. I didn't hear a voice, but it was clear to me—I need to do this and nothing else. I'm still called."

I also remind myself it happened to other men greater than I. As I read Spurgeon, he'd fall into these depressions. He said in his *Lectures to My Students,* "I would see myself going to some village in America." I said, "Don't bother, it's going to happen there too! It's not going to be any different than it was in London." It happens to other great men and women, and it will happen to us. I remind myself of that.

The third thing I would tell myself is that I have a good team of people around me on our staff. I tell them, "I am going to be in a below-water spot," and interestingly, I will usually find a like-hearted fellow who will say, "Me too. I'm kind of encouraged to know that you go through those times too." Happily they do not happen over long periods, and they don't necessarily come as one would expect. They come at surprising times. Spurgeon says, "I never did anything great that wasn't preceded by a time of depression." So he speaks of encouragement in it, knowing that it's going to lead to something. You know what, I'm not in his camp, but I've had that experience. Not always. I think his experience was that this usually happened. I can't say usually. But I've had it happen that when I pull out of it, there'll be a new vista. Like you pay the price for the mountains by going through the desert leading to them. Then once you're up there you think, "Oh, I'm so glad I stayed on the road and didn't pull over and stop too soon."

Fourth, I remind myself that difficult times are where we sharpen our sights for people in the real world who often live in those dry seasons. So in the depths, in the barren times, the Spirit of God hasn't necessarily lifted from us. And I think he resides within us, so thankfully we have his presence. I think he's quiet for whatever reasons, and he reminds us, "Without me you can do nothing," as Christ said in John 15. I think he really means *nothing.*

So I just try to stay faithful and do my work. I usually get quieter. Life isn't rosy and pretty and fun, and I say so. But I think that when I do come through it I'm able to draw on it and say, "It is past."

The three crucial points of my preaching are accuracy, clarity, and practicality. I want to be accurate with the text, clearly present it, and be practical so that people have something that they can live with and go on—which is where the illustrations and applications play a part. A lady mentioned to me, "You should mention one more. Add vulnerability." She said, "Your ministry is vulnerable." And I said, "Boy, are you perceptive! I'm going to remember that." When you're being vulnerable, you are able to go back and say, "If you only knew the barren days that led to this momentary or brief period of fruitfulness." I say so when it's barren. What do I do? I say, "This is a tough time." Sometimes I'm not out of it by Sunday, and I say to the folks, "It's been a tough week. I'm coming to you as a fellow struggler, needing healing and encouragement." And I find people have room for that.

Interviewer: Perhaps many welcome it.

Swindoll: Yes. I think they get the idea we are Wonder Woman or Superman and we never have those times. I find it not infrequent that I will talk about some struggle that I went through,

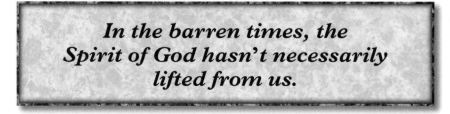

In the barren times, the Spirit of God hasn't necessarily lifted from us.

and those comments often become the catalyst or the crucible where something grows out of it—some deep ministry in someone's life.

I think we all have one thing in common, and that's pain. Joseph Parker used to tell young preachers, "Preach to broken hearts and you'll never lack for a congregation. There's one in every pew." I tell that to young ministers who I'm mentoring, to our interns, "You preach to broken hearts, you won't miss." I think we have to have a broader ministry than just brokenness, but I think we've got to remember that. So I think the barren times break us and bring us back to the foundation: God is good, his Word is true, be faithful.

God commands us to be faithful, he doesn't command us to be fruitful. Fruit happens, you know. Rosebuds don't scream, "I'm blooming! I'm blooming!" The old bush stays there, and every once in a while you'll be surprised with this brilliant flower that grows. My mother used to say that the roots grow deep when the winds are strong. So I think in the windy times, your roots grow deep. I think the Spirit of God is at work there too. It just isn't a fruitful time. Those are hard for us, especially we who like to produce.

Interviewer: As Spurgeon observed, times of greatest success often come after those barren times. Perhaps because those barren times drive us back to the utter dependence on God, he is able then to use us more.

Swindoll: Can we use the word recycle? We go back and we recycle; what goes around comes around. And having come through, we realize anew, "Lord, without you I can't pull this off." There was a time when I preached five times every Sunday—three times every morning and two times every night. I did four years of that, and it wasn't all peaches and cream. I remember leaning against the wall when the music minister and I were getting ready for the fifth (and last) service that Sunday. He said, "What have we done? What have we created?" I said, "Let's just stay at it. Don't analyze, just do it." He did, and we did it together. Then you drag yourself home at night, thinking, "Can I do this again?" You do. You're up for it again. I read Wesley and those guys who prepared on horseback and I think, "Oh, man, my deal is this—I've got it made!"

Interviewer: Let me shift directions. You mentioned preaching in series and how your books often emerge from these series. How much difference is there when you're going from a sermon series to a book? Do you use the sermons as the basis for chapters or do you essentially start over?

Swindoll: Those are two different questions. I'll answer the second one first. Yes, they become the basis of the chapter—a sermon becomes a chapter. How much difference? Contrary to what one may read in many books, with me there's a lot of difference. People do not read like they hear. Sermons that become books become boring books because the ear is very forgiving; the eye is much more exacting and demanding. I've really got convictions about this, and so a book becomes much more of an exacting task. Sir Francis Bacon said, "Speaking maketh a ready man, reading a broad man, writing an exact man." I love that quote and it's true. When I sit down to write, I have to rethink the precise wording, and often it will be far afield from the introduction I used for the sermon.

You and I have read sermons. We're not all as colorful as Spurgeon. I suppose his stuff could go right into books and he would hold us right in his hands. However, most of us are not that colorful. Though I do like to use word pictures and I do like analogies, I think when we are doing a book, we must realize eyes will be reading it.

I may be able to review and repeat in a series—and I think we should, because again, the ear is very forgiving and forgetful. So we need to remind people where we have been, especially if we're out of that series for a Sunday or two—for Mother's Day, seasons of the year, whatever. To come back into the series, we need to review, whereas the beginning of a chapter is not necessarily a good time to review where we've been in the previous chapters—occasionally it is. I usually do a little review toward the end of the book.

I also find that times change, and at the time I'm writing, other things are passionate to me and big on my list of important things than were in my sermons, so I will do some fresh work. I may also see that it doesn't look as good on paper as it did in a sermon, and I will change some points in there. I will rearrange, so if you were to read the transcript of the sermon or hear it over the radio—which is the actual delivery of what I do in Fullerton at the pulpit there—then read the book, you will say it isn't quite the same. It's deliberately not the same, because I have a passion for writing well, which requires that I do it with my own hands. I don't use a computer; I write longhand. I have a knot on my finger to prove it! I will actually write in script on a tablet. I give my secretary fifteen to eighteen pages of what I've done for the chapter, and it will mostly be brand new writing. But the homework will have been done, the spade work will have been done in the sermon.

Interviewer: You mentioned that you do use some notes when you preach. What kind of notes do you carry into the pulpit?

Swindoll: Fairly extensive. Within my Bible, I would put sheets of paper smaller than it is. When I open my Bible to the section I want to speak from, I'll just pull those notes out to the side and use them. I will use four or five sheets that size, single-spaced, and I type them myself. That I do on a typewriter, though if I'm traveling a lot, it will be handwritten like the books are. I would say the notes are fairly extensive—extensive enough for me to dip into them.

If I go to a conference and they've asked me to speak on grace, or they want me to speak on the joy of Christ in relation to *Laugh Again*, they often want me to do something out of Philippians. Then I will pull those notes from my sermons that I preached and I will have enough material there—with the reference works I've pulled them from—to preach a thirty- to forty-minute review. The notes prepare my mind for that; sometimes more or even less than others, depending on familiarity and how long ago I did it.

Interviewer: In your process of preparing the sermon itself, do you go to notes or do you spend time actually writing it out?

Swindoll: Manuscripting sermons? If I'm in a tough spot, I will manuscript it because, again, writing makes an exact man. I think if it doesn't make sense on paper, it's not going to make sense verbally. The discipline of writing it down will help disentangle your thoughts. I learned a little piece years ago: "Thoughts disentangle themselves over the lips and through the fingertips." Sometimes I will go down the hall to one of my friends on the staff and go into his study and say, "Can I have a few minutes? I want to talk this thing out. I want you to pick at the pieces or I want you to disagree with me. I want you to listen to this as if you were not a believer, you're not a follower. Tell me your reaction." That's always a good discipline; in fact, I don't think I do that enough.

When we write messages out, when we prepare messages, we need to have the guy in mind who's not in our camp. I'd say, "I'm going to say something Sunday that's going to be a little startling, so I want you to be startled right now. Tell me what your reaction is—it'll be good, it's a good exercise." Sometimes he'll say, "Man, I don't buy that for anything." So I ask, "If I said it more, would you buy it?" He says, "No." I ask, "Well, would you listen?" He answers, "Yeah, I'd listen, but you'd leave me disagreeing." I say, "That's okay. It's all right to disagree. Is it true to what it seems like the Scripture is teaching?" He says, "Yeah, but I'm not even sure I could agree with that right now." And I'll say, "That's good—just so I'm not far afield from what the Scripture is saying."

I'll tell you where I get nervous on things like this—when I'm out of my field. My field is the Scriptures and theology, and when I get into medicine, the world of sewing, or fields like psychology, when I get into realms where I'm disagreeing or picking at them, I need to have my homework very carefully done or I need

> *I want to help those people who are studying hard to stay in touch with the world that's really there.*

to tread softly. I need to do a disclaimer on the front end: "I'm not a medical doctor, but as I understand the body, this is the way it functions." I did that when I was in a series on the church and we were doing analogies—the Shepherd and the sheep, the Vine and the branches, the Head and the body—those word pictures. I got into the realm of the body and I realized I was getting pretty deep into cells and muscles and blood and organs. I needed to make sure, so I talked about it with a medical doctor friend of mine. That helped. I would have made a couple of mistakes that would have been embarrassing. Legal things is another area where I need to be careful that I've really thought it through. That's a matter of accuracy; you need to be accurate with information.

Interviewer: In addition to your pastorate in Fullerton, you will soon assume the presidency of Dallas Seminary. You will have some real influence on the training of young preachers in that role.

Swindoll: I hope so. That's what excites me.

Interviewer: What would you hope most for them, and how would you try to encourage them?

Swindoll: I would hope most that they would be able to connect with the real world and not preach to fellow theologians. I think it is easy for a graduate school that does good academic work to crank out academic, scholarly students of the Scriptures rather than realistic, practical-minded pastors. My hope is that the school will continue to train Bible-thinking men and women who do good work in the text. However, I hope to add a dimension of realism because my world is the real world—real people, real needs. I want to help those people who are studying hard to stay in touch with the world that's really there, not the world that's in the cloistered halls of the school.

I realize it's not a little Bible college, and I don't mean that to sound condescending; it is a graduate school of theology and I want it to remain that. I'm not excited by what percentage is going to Cambridge to get a Ph.D., because I think that's what the world is full of, and I would include in that even the academic world. I remember the genius of Peter Marshall who got his training and did his seminary work, but when he was through, he still connected with the John Doe's who were to meet their Master. I think that's what I want to do. I believe I'm able to make a contribution in that realm, because that's the world I plan to stay in. I will remain in the pulpit and—because the seminary has a provost who is an academician and has credibility and respect—I think both sides will work in the best interest of the students. I hope to be able to do that; time will tell.

November/December 1993

22

PREACHING AND THE POWER OF WORDS

Gardner C. Taylor

Often called the dean of Black preachers in the United States, Gardner C. Taylor has proclaimed the gospel for more than half a century in churches across the nation and around the globe. He is now pastor emeritus of the Concord Baptist Church of God in Christ, in Brooklyn, New York.

Interviewer: You've had a long and productive ministry. What part has preaching played in your ministry over the years?

Taylor: I came along at a time when preaching was really at the center of Protestant church life—and most assuredly of Black churches, African American churches. That may have been about all that was happening in most of them, but there was a great emphasis on it. I had the opportunity to grow up in that era, and then I was privileged—really privileged—to go to New York at a time when I found the greatest concentration of gifted preachers perhaps in the whole history of Christendom.

When you think of it, at one time Scherer, Buttrick, McCracken, Steven Wise the Jewish preacher, and Fulton Sheen were still at work. There were all of those men, and then there was a remarkable Jewish preacher in Brooklyn, Sidney Tidestky, and one superlative Black preacher, Sandy Ray. Adam Powell was more a political preacher, but he had a certain charisma and a certain force of power. To have been thrown into that environment is the greatest privilege I've had as a preacher. I had the opportunity to preach there and wander among those men.

There used to be a kind of Lenten circuit—Syracuse, Detroit, Buffalo, Niagara Falls, Cleveland. There would be noonday services—some of them for a week at Old Stone Church in Cleveland, some for one night in the week, but it was a circuit—and I was privileged to become a part of that. I remember Henry Heath Crain, the Detroit preacher, as being in that group. I had that advantage.

My father was a preacher, and a remarkable preacher, really. My father was not highly educated, but he read constantly. I remember some of what he was doing in Baton Rouge, which would have been in the '20s—he died in 1931. It fascinated me. I had that background before these other things happened; really, it was providential how I was thrown into situations.

M. E. Dodd was minister in First Baptist Church of Shreveport. Did you know I preached in his pulpit one night when he had a Bible conference? I had spoken on the radio to a Black convention which had been carried in Shreveport. I spoke in his church—it had to be before 1947—and Robert G. Lee was the other preacher there. It was remarkable in my years to have had that kind of exposure.

Preaching that excites and electrifies, elevates and edifies, does not seem to me to be nearly as much in vogue now as it was in earlier years. One of the problems—I discovered this in students—is what our schools are doing in terms of literature. One key to the pulpit is language. The beauty with which people have used language seems to have dropped out of our undergraduate schools. People who write plays use the language with much more vividness than those of us who preach; that's sad. Also, I think these playwrights and novelists are dealing with deeper matters of human life in ways we preachers seem often afraid to confront.

Interviewer: When you were in the pastorate, did you try to read certain things that helped you keep your language fresh?

Taylor: Yes, I did then and I still do read the book review section of the *New York Times* every week. I get the *New York Review of Books,* though I don't get a chance to read as many of the books as I ought. And I read the arts and leisure section of the *New York Times.*

While at Oberlin College, I read almost every issue and almost every word of the *Christian Century Pulpit.* Now it has declined, but then it was the definitive thing. At that time, it had Scherer writing, Frederick Norwood the Australian preacher, Leslie Weatherhead, Clarence McCartney—people like that. I guess I was fascinated, and I'm sure a lot of their thought forms passed on to me almost without my awareness.

Interviewer: New York City had a rainbow of outstanding preachers in the early years of your ministry. Did you find having that kind of environment influenced your own preaching?

Taylor: Oh yes, I'm sure of that. I admired Scherer a great deal. He had a gift for metaphor which belonged to something almost native to my own background, and it was his preaching

> *One key to the pulpit is language. I think our preachers ought to seek to clothe the gospel in as worthy a language as they can find for it.*

which gave me a certain endorsement for what came naturally with me. I took a course with him at Union Seminary, and I came to know him. He preached for me in the Concord pulpit. But the atmosphere couldn't help affecting one, whether you had an interest in preaching or if you only wanted to hear preaching. I felt greatly privileged and honored to be in their company. I still do.

Interviewer: Besides those you've already mentioned, were there some others who had a lot of influence on you?

Taylor: Yes, James Stewart's work. I once had a conversation with Stewart. He and I talked about A. J. Gossip's preaching, and I'll never forget his phrase. He said Gossip's preaching was like, as he put it in his Scottish way, "a river at spate." I'll never forget that phrase.

Clarence McCartney was a magnificent preacher. He was Harry Emerson Fosdick's principal opponent, I guess. Magnificent preacher. McCartney had a remarkable gift for bringing the Bible and biblical characters into focus in a life-giving way. I had a wonderful colleague in Brooklyn, Sandy Ray; it was sad that our fractures of race did not open him to the wider Christian community. He served the Cornerstone Baptist Church in Brooklyn. Wonderful. He had a gift.

Interviewer: How has preaching changed during your lifetime? Has your preaching changed?

Taylor: I hope it has. I hope it's changed for the better, though sometimes I'm not sure about that. In my case, my imaginative powers are not like they were. I never could memorize, but I could carry phrases. I don't have that ability as I once had.

I tell my students they ought to be open to things after periods of barrenness. I saw a documentary on Miles Davis, the trumpeter, and he was saying that for five years he lost the sound of his music. I talked with some jazz musicians about this, and they said he did lose it. Then Davis started producing a new sound—what they call "cool jazz"—which is out of my area, but I get great lessons from this. Something inside Davis curled up and changed and there was this emptiness, but then a new thing came.

I have discovered barren periods in my preaching. I guess everyone does. My wife calls them preaching plateaus. I go through them. I have discovered that each plateau is a kind of preparatory period—if we allow it to be—for a new burst of energy and insight.

Language has become the mode of expressing the gospel. As Scherer said in his Beecher Lectures, "Words are the weapons of our warfare." I've often said it seems to me I could have invented a better way to transmit this gospel than preaching. It's so insubstantial, in a way of speaking, yet the Lord has done it. The mode of expression today has become more metallic.

Interviewer: What do you mean by that?

Taylor: I mean a certain flat, pedestrian language that does not fire the imagination. It is not gripping. Preaching may be confrontational sometimes, certainly exhortatory, but it should have an added sense of the majesty of life, the glory of its possibilities, and the greatness and glory of God. It's saying something, but it's saying something in a glorious way. I don't hear that in preaching as much as I'd like.

Another remarkable preacher I will never forget—when we were in Orlando for the National Conference on Preaching, that sermon by James Earl Massey on Jacob was a tremendous thing. I don't hear enough of that—the drawing forth of these ancient characters and giving them contemporary meaning. What I hear is jazzy. I think language ought to be crisp and contemporary. This kind of jazzy, camp language in the pulpit bothers me. I guess it's a part of me being old and all!

Interviewer: One of the interesting things that relates to language in the last few years among preachers is a new attention on narrative and stories. It seems to me that one of the great elements of African American preaching has always been the story, the vivid image.

Taylor: No question; always has been. Coming really out of our background—or most of it—is a subconscious stream of story. In the villages of Africa, the *griot* was the person who through story carried the myths of the tribe from generation to generation. He was storyteller and historian to an oral people who had no written works. Also, wherever people have known oppression there comes a kind of vividness, a kind of apocalyptic quality to their thinking, a gift for indirect statement.

There was something in the story about my people who came out of slavery which had in it a mixture of humility, earthiness, mysticism, and a beauty of language. I heard it as a boy, and though this was passed on orally from one generation to the other, that did not diminish its beauty. I remember some of the praises of African American deacons or other men praying: "We come before you, knee bent and body bowed; our hearts below our knees and our knees in some lonesome valley." I'm thankful that I have been heir to that.

I think my own preaching was affected, and it should have been, by the civil rights era. Sometimes I have the feeling about African American preaching that we too often, for too long, were otherworldly and then became too much this-worldly, when it ought to be a mixture.

Interviewer: You speak to pastors all over the country, and I'm sure you have opportunity to talk with many and hear some of the things on their hearts. What do you think are some of the greatest concerns pastors are feeling these days, particularly in areas that would relate to preaching and worship?

Taylor: I think many preachers are overpowered by this society. When I went to New York, the *Times* on Monday would carry excerpts from Sunday sermons. There has been this draining out of religion from American life, unless it has an angle to it, or is off-center. Uncertainty about the structures of the society seems to be clear and powerful, but here we are. Yet this is what Jesus said to his disciples, "I have sent you forth, sheep in the midst of wolves." When those disciples looked at the magnificence of Herod's temple, they oohed and aahed. Preachers are not to scorn the culture; there are notable and wonderful things about it. They are to realize that culture is human, temporal, passing. We are to address our culture as a part of it and yet not a part of it, and to address it with that kind of authority, not arrogance, that comes to one who believes that he or she is an emissary of a kingdom that will outlast all kingdoms.

There's a great hurting among pastors. Owen Cooper lived in Yazoo City, Mississippi—a remarkable man. He was one of the few laypersons who was president of the Southern Baptist Convention. Cooper sent an open letter to Southern Baptist laymen urging them—pleading with them, really—to allow their pastors to preach to them the whole dimension of the Bible. For whatever reason, many of us are afraid to deal with the whole sweep of the gospel. I'm not just talking about race now. I'm talking also about greed. I'm talking about the private and public immorality of corruption in our public life. This has something to do with the moral health of the nation, and by the living God, I believe the gospel has something to say to it. I'm not talking

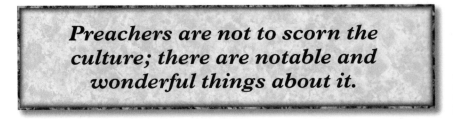

Preachers are not to scorn the culture; there are notable and wonderful things about it.

about any partisan issue; I'm talking about the spiritual welfare of a nation, and therefore, the spiritual welfare of individuals. I'm talking about setting our human lives within the light of the gospel; that's what I'm doing.

I was at William Jewell College when a man asked me, "You preach this in your church?" I said, "Yeah." He said, "I couldn't do that. People would think I was getting to be too highfalutin." We were not talking about race.

Interviewer: Do you think pastors sometimes underestimate their congregations?

Taylor: Yes, no question about it. I tell my students that *they* think there are certain things they can't preach to people. Well, almost any congregation, no matter where it is, has about the same color of intelligence. It may not have the same trim. I tell the students that congregations can get it, if pastors have got it. I tell them, if you're not quite clear on what you're dealing with, they may not get it. Sometimes, though, even that is rescued by the Holy Spirit and congregations get it even though you don't know what you're talking about! But you ought not to presume God's rescue. Yes, I think pastors sometimes underestimate their congregations, no question about it.

Interviewer: What counsel would you offer to young preachers?

Taylor: The first thing I would tell a young preacher is to be available for what the Lord wants to do in his or her life—have an openness, a readiness. I don't think there's anything to substitute for that.

I would also suggest that there be a balance between spirituality and intellectuality. Be sure neither one dominates the other; if one does, it should be spirituality—with intellectuality in close contest. I'm at Princeton now, and there's a pietistic thing—which I admire—but also a suspicion of learning. I think it goes back to the old Princeton controversy. I say to the students that true spirituality is not embarrassed by anything intellectual. True spirituality can handle anything; you don't have to suppress it. True intellectuality is not compromised by spirituality.

I spent a morning with Albert Einstein. Unbelievable! I was preaching at the Princeton Presbyterian Church, traveling there on the train every day. A gentleman who came to the service asked, "Would you like to meet Albert Einstein?" I said, "Would I like to?!" He told me, "It means you would have to come down on an earlier train." I said, "I'll stay up all night!" I did go down and had a talk with him. During the course of our conversation—he was not a person of great spiritual design—Einstein said the theory of relativity was the greatest thought that ever came to him. What does he mean by "came" to him? It must have arrived from somewhere outside himself, which means that we are not in this alone.

There's a great story about John Wesley. A woman is supposed to have said to him, "You know, Mr. Wesley, the Lord does not need all of your Oxford education." He said, "Of course not, madam. He doesn't need your ignorance, either." I wouldn't want to say that one ought to cultivate the mind and neglect the heart.

Also, I think our preachers ought to seek to clothe the gospel in as worthy a language as they can find for it. I would want to say something about their prayer life. In New York, I became a member of the board of education and got into New York politics and all that kind of thing. My wife said to me, "You're going to wither in your work. Your preaching is getting very thin." I have never heard a thing that stung me about my work like that did! But the Lord quickly got me out of there when Nelson Rockefeller dismissed the whole board. My wife claimed I was the

Jonah! I may have been, I don't know. He put us all out. I agree that we ought to give large amounts of time for our own spiritual nurturing.

My own people used to talk about looking into the Rock. Sometimes you'd come upon them and they'd just be sitting. This solitariness, and this willingness to be alone, to reflect, to brood, and to let the Spirit have its play upon our lives—these are things I think we miss, partly because we don't have confidence that what we do is authentic enough. We feel we have to justify ourselves in the society and in the community by doing a lot of other things that we are not called to do.

I come back to that matter of identity—recognizing our calling, recognizing its significance, not presuming upon it, and—for heaven's sake—trying not to be arrogant about it. In Lewis Drummond's work on Charles Spurgeon, there appeared to be a certain arrogance about Spurgeon, and it may have been unbecoming. I know it was in Joseph Parker. It was in Paul Scherer. It was in George Buttrick.

I talked with a student of Buttrick and asked what was the characteristic about him that the student saw most clearly. Buttrick was a remarkable preacher—he was a humble man—but sometimes his awareness of his gifts got ahead of his humility. Yet these men also had a sense of what they did, and that gave them a sense of who they were. You see this in Paul, his awareness of who he was. He said, "I shouldn't do this, but I'm going on a little longer with it." It's a wonderful kind of way to look at things.

I would hope that more of our pastors would consider longer pastorates. Sure, pastorates can be too long, and I know that very well. When I first went to my pulpit the men who were my deacons were like fathers to me and they surrounded me with prayer. Sometimes their faces pass before me now in the evening and in the day too. They became as brothers, and then at last as sons. There's something to be said for a continuing pastoral relationship; no question about it. But it can get too long and people can long for something new. Here one has to consult the Holy Spirit and look for guidance in that matter.

Interviewer: Those pastors who really changed their cities almost invariably are those who have had extended pastoral service.

Taylor: I'm sure you can study successful preachers—Beecher, Fosdick, Truett, Spurgeon, Parker—and see that all of them had long pastorates. I remind young preachers of this, particularly young African American preachers, because with us there is a new materialism—I wish I could call it by some other name, but I'm close to the truth. And people do not turn themselves over to strangers; nobody does. Unless you're claiming that because you are a minister of the gospel and therefore have the divine right for people to turn their lives over to you, it's presumptuous to think people will hastily turn over their lives to you. People don't do that. It takes time to develop relationships of trust and love and mutual interest. I would urge pastors to at least consider longer periods of service.

January/February 1994

Preaching Is Not Just Story, It's Image

Warren Wiersbe

Books by Warren Wiersbe, one of the most prolific writers among evangelicals, are eagerly awaited by preachers as well as laypersons who admire his insightful interpretation and useful application of Scripture.

Born in the Chicago area and raised in the industrial area of northern Indiana, Wiersbe made his commitment to Christ at a Youth for Christ rally where Billy Graham was the speaker. He attended Northern Baptist Seminary, then joined the Youth for Christ staff. After two pastorates, including the Moody Church in Chicago (from 1971 to 1978), Wiersbe became featured speaker for the *Back to the Bible* radio broadcast, which he continued until 1989.

Today Wiersbe serves as Senior Contributing Editor for Baker Book House and as Distinguished Professor of Preaching at Grand Rapids Baptist Seminary.

216

Interviewer: You have spoken a good deal about the importance of doctrinal preaching. That's an area that increasingly seems to be overlooked. Tell me what you mean by doctrinal preaching and why you think it is such an important need within the church.

Wiersbe: Of course all preaching ought to be doctrinal. Any preaching that's not based on Bible doctrine is questionable. The doctrinal sermon is one that focuses primarily on the explanation and application of a specific doctrine—justification by faith, adoption, the virgin birth, whatever it may be.

It's important because our faith is based on doctrine. Our faith is based on historical fact. Second Timothy 3:16, the classic passage, says that Scripture is profitable for teaching or doctrine. It's good to know what you believe and why you believe it—that's what people need today.

Interviewer: How would you compare or contrast doctrinal preaching with a typical expository sermon?

Wiersbe: There need not be contrast. You could take a key passage and develop a doctrine. You could develop the theme of justification by faith from Romans 4, and it could be expository; or you could develop the theme of regeneration from John 3. But often doctrinal sermons are more on the topical side, because you could go on for a long time on justification by faith! But you should take one aspect of a theme from the text, and the sermon need not be topical. It could be expository.

Interviewer: When you were in the pastorate, what was the nature of your own preaching ministry? Did you preach in series or otherwise plan your preaching schedule?

Wiersbe: In the first church I pastored (when I was a seminary student and pastor at the same time), I had no system. I should have had one, but no one told me exactly how to do it. When I was at Calvary Baptist in Covington, Kentucky, I always preached a series of sermons. I would work my way through a book. The mistake I made at Calvary was to let the series run too long. This was the thing you were supposed to do—to be able to say to your pastor friends, "I just finished two years in Philippians!" Spurgeon talked about the man who spent eight years in Hebrews. The preacher got to the closing chapter where it says, "Suffer this word of exhortation," and Spurgeon said, "They suffered." That's what I am afraid I was doing.

While I was at Moody Church, I learned that the attention span in the big city is not quite that long. So I limited a series to perhaps three months, and then took a break. When I did Acts, for example, I preached from Acts for three months, then took a break. Without telling people, I often followed the Christian church calendar. I recommend this. I didn't announce it; it would have scared some of them! But I watched the calendar so that I was always ready for a break in my series at the Lenten season. I wanted to have the church prepared for Good Friday and Easter. I would prepare for the Advent season in the same way.

Interviewer: How did you know what you ought to be preaching? In selecting a series, how did you go about evaluating that?

Wiersbe: In planning a series, I would try to say to myself, "What is it that excites me?" because I can do my best with that which excites me. I'd ask, "Where is the state of the church? Do we need the outreach emphasis with Acts? Do we need the faith emphasis of Hebrews 11? What does this church need at this point?" This is where pastoral work comes in. We must know our people. We should also listen to the people. When I was at Moody Church, I came to a point one year where I was stymied. I didn't know what to plan for the fall messages, and I always

> *When I preach publicly, I preach to one person because the Word is for individuals.*

tried to plan six months in advance so that the staff knew where we were going. At an elders' meeting, I confessed my perplexity. I said, "Brethren, I've been here several years now—I don't know what to do." One of the elders spoke up and said, "Have you ever considered doing a series on suffering?" I said, "No, but I know that a lot of our people are going through difficulty." He said, "Pray about it." So I did, and the Lord gave me seven messages on suffering which were greatly used by God to help both the church and the pastor. The series eventually developed into my book, *Why Us? When Bad Things Happen to God's People.* In that situation, the series idea grew out of the eldership.

I've always tried to balance the series. If I'm doing the Old Testament in the morning, I want to do something from the New Testament at night. I always felt that the evening service should not be a duplication of the morning service. We always had more music, more participation, and a different kind of a message.

How do you evaluate it? I guess the general growth and development of the church. You preach by faith. Somebody described preaching—radio preaching in particular—as a doctor standing at the top of the Empire State Building with an eyedropper in his hand, trying to get medicine into somebody's eye down there on the street. It's hard to know what is being accomplished. But people say to you, "The messages in this series are helping me." That encourages you.

Interviewer: Talking about radio preaching, it strikes me that it would be very different from preaching to a local congregation—preaching Sunday by Sunday to a very different kind of audience.

Wiersbe: At *Back to the Bible,* it was studio preaching; there was no visible audience. I wanted them to change. One of my early suggestions was, "Let's change and do what Chuck Swindoll is doing and others are doing; let's tape it from a live situation." This has a number of advantages: First, it's much easier to preach to a live congregation than it is in a studio. Second, you can use humor—you can't do that in the studio; they don't know you're being funny. They take you seriously. But if they hear the laughter coming from the congregation, they say, "Hey, it was funny!" But the board preferred not to change. They said, "Ours is a studio ministry." So the difficulty of the studio ministry is you must be very careful what you say and how you say it. The listeners cannot see your face. They don't know what your expression is. You've got to imagine one person listening, not a big congregation.

Actually, when you preach to a congregation, you don't preach to a congregation but to an assembly of *individuals*. When I preach publicly, I preach to one person because the Word is for individuals. The radio preacher who talks about "people out in radio land" invites everybody to turn the radio off, because there are no "people"—only individuals—it's a woman ironing clothes, or a truck driver on the road; you're talking to an individual. You should do that, I think, in pulpit ministry rather than talk to a crowd. How do you preach to a crowd? Crowds don't do anything; individuals do. I like Phillips Brooks's definition of preaching: "The communication of divine truth through human personality." We preach as individuals to individuals.

Interviewer: Through your books and your radio ministry, you have been a favorite of many preachers. Many have drawn encouragement and ideas from you. Who were the folks you drew encouragement from or who you enjoyed listening to or reading?

Wiersbe: I have two sets of homiletical heroes—the dead and the living. Among the dead, Campbell Morgan is a hero—his sermons and books have been a great encouragement to me and, of course, Spurgeon, but for a different reason. I read Spurgeon not as a preacher or a homiletician, but as a sinner just needing God's grace. Many times I will come home from church on Sunday morning, and while my wife is getting dinner ready, I'll just sit down and read one of Spurgeon's sermons. It does my soul good. A relatively neglected preacher, George Morrison, had a great influence on me. He pastored the University Presbyterian Church in Glasgow. An hour before the service, the line of people in front of the church would reach around the block. He published many books of sermons—they're out of print, as many good books are—but he had a poetic gift in his preaching.

You must know this about me—my early preaching ministry was very analytical, very content centered. In these recent years, I have moved away from the emphasis on *content* to *intent*. I did not agree with his theology, but Harry Emerson Fosdick was right when he said, "The purpose of preaching is not to explain a subject, but to achieve an object." So I've moved more into that, plus I use more imagination. For several years, I've been working on a book on imagination in preaching—not how to think up illustrations and clever titles, but about the theology and psychology of imagination. You read the Bible and it's a picture book. It's not a book of doctrine, or even a theology book; it's a picture book, but we don't preach that way. There's a lot of material available on imagination. The secular philosophers and semanticists have been doing a great deal of study on metaphor. You read Isaiah and see what a master he was of the imaginative. I was reading Hosea the other day, and there must be thirty or forty similes and metaphors in that one book. So when I prepare a sermon, the first question I ask is, "What does the text say?" Then I ask, "How does it say it?" I used to skip that. "Is my text a poem, a proverb, a narrative, a story, a parable? What kind of literature is it—and why did the writer use this approach?" Bible preachers preached in that mode; why don't we? We analyze everything to death.

Interviewer: The whole contemporary movement emphasizes narrative in preaching—how do you react to that?

Wiersbe: Narrative preaching must not be simply retelling an old story in modern dress. Preaching is not just story, it's *image*. Paul in his Epistles used dozens of images of the church.

> *Narrative preaching must not be simply retelling an old story in modern dress. Preaching is not just story, it's* image.

Peter did the same thing. Instead of giving a long speech about separation, Peter says, "You are pilgrims and aliens in this world." Symbolism has a way of growing. You take an image— it applies to my age, it applied to the age Peter wrote to, it will apply to the church fifty years from now. So imagery has a way of giving truth prominence of expression, but freedom to expand.

Narrative is good, but some preachers have made the mistake of thinking, "All you do is tell a story." Then you become an evangelical Garrison Keillor, for example. Keillor is a master at telling stories, but I think preaching is much more than that.

Interviewer: Tell me about the contemporary models. Are there some contemporary folks that you like?

Wiersbe: Unfortunately, I don't get to hear many preachers. I do read them. He's dead now, but J. Wallace Hamilton was really a creative preacher, and his books are worth reading. I appreciate Chuck Swindoll's preaching; he has a warm, practical touch. I appreciate David Jeremiah in El Cajon, California. We have been together in conferences and I thoroughly enjoy his messages—biblical, contemporary, up-to-date. The old Youth for Christ slogan, "Geared to the times, but anchored to the Rock," sure applies to preaching. I wish I could get to hear more people, but I don't.

Of course we've all heard the greats. W. A. Criswell has been a great blessing to so many of us. I remember listening to R. G. Lee and saying, "I'll never preach again. There's no sense my even getting up. I'll never preach again." A. W. Tozer was a great blessing to me. I heard him preach many times. I also liked Vance Havner—I miss him, I really do. We needed him, and I always enjoyed hearing him. These are very special people. There will never be another W. A. Criswell. There will never be another Vance Havner.

Most of what we know about preaching comes through the printed page rather than the spoken word. I've been with Stuart Briscoe in conferences. His ministry always blesses me, and I think over the years Stuart's ministry of the Word has changed. He seems to be moving more toward the practical and imaginative in his sermons rather than the didactic and analysis.

I think sermons are getting shorter. Bob Cook used to tell us in Youth for Christ that a sermon does not have to be eternal to be immortal. Sermons are getting shorter, preaching is getting more personal, and the preacher has to be more open and more transparent. The day is over when people simply accept the authority of the text; they also need to be assured of the authority of the preacher. We need to be more transparent. When I started my ministry over forty years ago, a preacher would not tell publicly about some dumb thing he did that week, but now many preachers do it. I think preaching is changing for the better if what I read is what people are hearing. I think there are some fine young preachers coming along. I won't name them, but I'm grateful for what God is doing in and through them. They're better trained than I was when I got started, and they have better tools.

Interviewer: If you had one word for preachers that you could pass along to them—encouragement, advice, or counseling—what would you say?

Wiersbe: The same thing I heard W. A. Criswell say on the radio the other day: Give your morning to God. Start your day with the Lord. Ministry is not what we *do* so much as what we *are*. Phillips Brooks said that when God wants to make a sermon, he first makes a preacher. The most important part of a

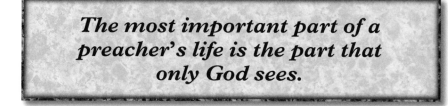

The most important part of a preacher's life is the part that only God sees.

preacher's life is the part that only God sees—the time alone with God, when you're not sermonizing, when you're not preparing for public ministry, when you are a sinner worshiping a holy God. "Without me you can do nothing," said Jesus. He didn't say, "Without me you are handicapped." So I would say to every preacher: Cultivate your spiritual roots and start each day with the Lord.

Let God build you. I learned early in my life that I'm not an evangelist. I admire these people who can read John 3:16, make three or four points, tell two or three stories, and people get saved. I can't do that. That's not my calling. I'm doing the thing God called me to do, but if I didn't spend time every day with the Lord and let him build into me what he wants, I couldn't do what he wants. So my word would be that: Cultivate your spiritual roots.

Interviewer: Pastors have told me this is one of the toughest disciplines for them.

Wiersbe: But it's a lot tougher if you *don't* do it! When we were at Moody Church in Chicago, I jealously guarded my Saturday evenings. There was a great deal of "evangelical nightlife" in Chicago. We could have gone to a lot of places, enjoying a lot of things, but on Saturday evenings, I would go to my study at home and prepare myself for the Lord's Day. I would think through my message and talk to God. I would make sure there was nothing in the sermon that was not real to me. I would prepare my pulpit prayer. I wouldn't write it out, but I would prepare it so that I wasn't praying the same thing every week. Because I'm an early riser and I spend time early in the morning with the Lord, we don't do a lot of late-night fellowshiping. Yes, it's a price to pay, but I wouldn't want it any other way. When you make preaching the priority of your ministry, everything else falls into place. You don't waste time here and there. You can't go to every meeting.

May/June 1992

PREACHING
TO THE BAPTIZED

William Willimon

William Willimon, dean of the chapel at Duke University, is one of the most prolific authors in American Christianity. His books consistently offer insights worth reading. He is also a gifted and challenging preacher who is widely sought for conferences and programs throughout the United States.

Interviewer: In your book *Peculiar Speech: Preaching to the Baptized* you talk about the distinctiveness of the preaching task within the Christian community. Describe what you mean by "preaching to the baptized" and what it is that makes this a unique form of discourse.

Willimon: The book sort of begins after a throwaway remark by Walter Brueggeman that a lot of preaching he heard was not addressed to anybody specifically—least of all to the baptized—and that hit a chord with me. I'm afraid that a lot of preaching that I was trained to preach had as a kind of underlying assump-

225

tion that good communication is addressed to nine out of ten average Americans—that the best ideas are those that have the most universal applicability. This is the sermon that starts out, "Have you ever been depressed? Have you ever felt down?" The response is, "Of course. Everybody's felt like that." Then the sermon goes on: "Okay, great. And surprise—the Bible has something about that, and now I'm going to apply that to the general human situation."

Well, there are some assumptions behind that. One is that there is something called a general human situation. That is really being challenged now by feminists and others who've answered, when somebody says, "This is human nature," or, "This is the human condition," that you're hearing a testimony of a people who just happen to be on top and in charge and think that everybody else has got to think like they do because they're on top.

Also, it is not fair to what I call the rather arrogant, imperialistic claims of the Bible. I don't know what the human condition is until the Bible tells me. I mean, why would depression be an interesting thing to worry about? The fact that nine out of ten Americans feel depressed may or may not be interesting, but where did we even get the word *depression*? Who told us it was bad to be depressed?

My book is called *Peculiar Speech*, and I'm interested in how the Bible engenders a kind of peculiar way of talking about the world. More than that, the book is addressed to people who've been baptized. That is, people who have signed on board to live their lives on the basis of these stories—on the basis of this weird account of the way the world is put together. That makes a difference.

Interviewer: One of the things preachers increasingly are told is to speak language that people can understand, not the in-house lingo or terminology that only a small elite will understand. You seem to be speaking counter to that—saying that there are some things that you have to be a part of the group to understand, and it's appropriate to use such language.

Willimon: I'm not defending nonbiblical ways of talking; most people don't know what words like *redemption, atonement,* and *sanctification* mean. But, of course, Jesus never used any of those words, either. So he is a model, but I think we contemporary

Christian communicators have not given the gospel credit for how odd it is, and how we don't really know what these everyday words that everybody thinks they already understand are—words like *the poor, child, Caesar, the world*—until the gospel tells us, because the gospel has some very peculiar things to say about these words.

In the Gospels, for instance, there is this constant struggle going on to reinterpret words. When they say, "Hey, you're the Messiah," Jesus said, "Yeah, and I'm getting ready to go suffer and die." And they say, "Wait, if the first point is true, that you're the Messiah, what are you doing suffering and dying?" Well, Jesus is already assaulting their notions of messiahship, and this happens all the time.

Or when Jesus says, "Hey, blessed are the poor." Well, if we don't do a double take on that one, we've just become incredibly dull. I think it's meant to say some weird things about being poor. I think it's meant to say some weird things about the kingdom. I guess I wanted to say there are real limits to talking so you can be understood, and I'm really bothered—we preachers should be bothered—if people come out every Sunday and say, "Oh, thank you for making it so understandable."

It's like a student once said to me, "The trouble with you preachers is you're always making things seem complicated." And I said, "Really?" He said, "Yeah, we ask you a simple question and get back this long, tortured answer." I said, "Well, if that's true, I'm probably being more of a professor than a preacher." And I added, "The nice thing is the gospel is very, very simple." He said, "Like what?" I said, "Like, go sell everything you've got, give it to the poor—then you'll have it. What could be more simple?" That's just the simplest thing in the world to understand. Which reminds me that the gospel is not an intellectual dilemma as much as it is a discipleship dilemma.

Maybe that gets us to the heart of the difficulty of the gospel. It's not that we're twentieth-century people, but that we're idolaters. Of course when I say that, you say, "Well, yeah, so were they." Well, we are and I think there's almost an arrogant modernism which says, "We've got this big, big problem with the gospel because we're so modern and sophisticated and they weren't." Well, a text like the one about the rich young ruler reminds me: We're caught in the same bind they were in and the preacher should help me to see that.

Interviewer: Leslie Newbigin says that Western society increasingly is a foreign mission field. I think you can certainly make the case that many of our congregations are mission fields. Is there a danger in preaching to the baptized without some awareness that, at the same time we are preaching to the baptized, we may also be preaching to the unconverted?

Willimon: Absolutely. I resonate with Leslie Newbigin. I'd put it this way—that the people we talk to are not only the baptized, but they are those willing to be baptized who may have already been baptized. Like when Paul says to the Romans, "Hey, what's this? Shouldn't we sin all the more so that grace can

> *The gospel is not an intellectual dilemma as much as it is a discipleship dilemma.*

abound all the more? Don't you know that you've been baptized? You're dead. You're dead to your sin; you're alive to Christ." Well, Paul wouldn't have had to write all that stuff to them if it had become clear to them in their baptism. And you love the way he goes back and kind of reminds them, "Hey, wait—you're talking out of your head. You're baptized. You can't talk like that anymore." Well, that's preaching to the baptized too—those who are in the process of being converted.

I really think mainline Protestantism has got to talk a lot more about conversion. Of course, I also think—and maybe this is the Wesleyan coming out in me—American evangelicalism has erred in thinking of conversion as a kind of one-time, momentary jerk of the Spirit. I'd like to say, "Hey, I have to get cleaned up all the time. I have to be baptized and washed and dead and raised, again and again." I think of it as a kind of lifetime process. I guess by saying "preaching to the baptized," one thing I'm trying to convey is that I want to give dignity to baptism, and maybe for the reasons you mentioned. When people come out and say, "That is the most outrageous, shocking, confusing thing I have ever heard; I just find that shocking," I want to say to them, "Well, what did you expect? It's called church; it's called the gospel. I didn't invite you down here. I didn't call you to follow Jesus— Jesus did. I didn't want you as a disciple. Did somebody tell you this was going to be easy? Hey, you're baptized for heaven's sake! This stuff is big. It's large; it's confusing." In that way, I want to give dignity to their baptism.

I think that one of the greatest things preachers can do is to take their miserable little lives and make them cosmic—make them large, and give dignity to what they're doing. I sometimes say it at my place: "You know, I'm sorry, boys and girls, you couldn't have heard this anywhere else but here. You had to put on a coat and tie and get all dressed up and come down here on a Sunday morning at an inconvenient hour to hear this. This is stuff they ain't talking about anywhere else—it's just for you." In a way I want to try to say, "Being Christian is not to be boring and bourgeois with a station wagon. Being Christian is an adventure."

I remember the great evangelical madman, Tony Campolo, preached for us one Sunday. He preached forty-five minutes; he screamed and he danced. Then we had the Duke Dance Ensemble come and portray the psalm with their bodies, and somebody had a timpani drum and started beating on it for the anthem—this weird contemporary anthem. We just kind of walked out reeling and shaking. This kid told me, "I invited a friend of mine who had been to church as a kid but he hadn't come in a long time. I'd been on him for a long time, 'Come to church with me,' and so I brought him to church. I was so proud because as he walked from the church he said, 'Wow, what was that?' I lied. I said it was a typical Sunday; that that's what we do when we get together." I think what I heard that kid saying was, "I was really proud to be a Christian. It was interesting, it was challenging, and it was big."

One thing that really concerns me about a lot of preaching that I hear called evangelical is they act as if the goal is to make the gospel as small as possible. We used to tell an old joke about the evangelist saying, "Come down to the altar and accept Jesus as your Savior." Nobody comes. He tries again, "If you want to lead a better life, come down to the altar." Nobody comes. Again he tries, "If you love your mother, come down to the altar." And it has kind of that quality—you know, get it down to a bumper sticker, or what you can put on a sign in front of the church.

Then I say maybe the best evangelism is that which is larger—it's just big—where people come forward and say, "I have my college degree and I'm a very intelligent person, and I've never heard anything like this before. I'm having difficulty with what you just said." I'd love a race of preachers who take that as a high compliment and say, "Of course, as if you could possibly understand after visiting only one time. How much are you willing to pay for this? Are you interested? We do have a class."

To me, that would be fairer to the gospel than bragging, "I am proud to say I have never ever confused anybody in a sermon. I have gotten it down now to where they'll sit there and say, 'That's what I've always thought. Yeah, thank you for helping me name that.'" By the way, that's liberal Protestantism, which has bled in now to the church growth movement in some of its aspects, and I think it's ugly. I think that's cheap, because it's not fair to the gospel. The gospel is not what you've always thought.

September/October 1993

PREACHING IN A
CHANGING CULTURE

Ed Young

Ed Young is senior pastor of one of America's largest and fastest-growing congregations, the Second Baptist Church of Houston, Texas. Located on a large, contemporary campus in suburban Houston featured in a full-page illustration in *USA Today,* the church offers a model of reaching and involving young and median adults. Young is seen weekly on a nationally televised program featuring the worship service at Second Baptist.

Interviewer: Your book *Been There, Done That, Now What?* deals with the increasing sense of life's meaninglessness and the lack of value of life that seems so prevalent in American culture today. As you minister to your own congregation, do you find that to be a common attitude, particularly with baby boomers?

Young: Absolutely, it's common with boomers *and* busters. I think that in different ways everyone is looking for meaning, and they try many different channels. In reading the Book of Eccle-

231

siastes, I realized this was Solomon also—been there, done that, now what? Solomon wrote three books in the Bible. Song of Solomon, a romantic book, is filled with chemistry, love, and great words that sizzle of his first love. Then he wrote Proverbs as a middle-aged man, successful. Been there, done that. Then he reveals his inner heart and soul—perhaps his journal or his spiritual autobiography—and that's the Book of Ecclesiastes. The end result is that he looks back and says, "I have lived a life under the sun." It was a life of emptiness, a life void of meaning. Solomon, who was the wealthiest person who ever lived and evidently one of the most brilliant individuals who has ever lived, gets to the end of his life—after he's accomplished all that he'd accomplished—and he says it's all empty. It's all futility. It's all vanity. And he says, "Now what, now what? What's it all about, what did it mean?" He missed the meaning of life.

Interviewer: Why do people feel that way today?

Young: I think they're trying the same thing Solomon did. Many people are pursuing pleasure; they're hedonists. A lot of people are pursuing materialism; they're pursuing wealth. Someone just told me that one who is wealthy has one, and only one, advantage over those of us who are not wealthy. I asked, "What is it?" He replied, "They know wealth will not bring happiness." I think people are trying the same things. There's nothing new under the sun and Solomon lived an under-the-sun lifestyle. In doing so, he cut off the tie with God that he had early in his life.

No one else in history that I know of was told by God, "Name it and you have it," basically given a blank check. Solomon asked for wisdom, and God was so pleased that he gave him wisdom and honor and wealth. That's the way God does things, you know. When God's pleased, he gives us more than we ask for. But somewhere along the way with building the temple, Solomon—who I believe went through all the rituals of worship and all the paths of being a religious man, a God-fearing man— somewhere along the way, he sold out to this world's structure and this world's system. We've seen that sellout happen in America in our own lifetime.

Interviewer: You're pastor of a major church that has obviously experienced tremendous growth. What part has preaching played in the development of Second Baptist?

Young: I think preaching is vital, I really do. First of all, I think worship is vital, and preaching is a part of worship. It's where the family meets, where they give praise to God, where there is celebration, where there is testimony, where the Word of God is read, and where the Word of God is proclaimed. It's a vital part of worship. It's amazing to me how sometimes we can take the Bible and exegete it and teach it and preach it—and make it boring.

To me, good preaching involves a variety of approaches. I think all preaching, by definition, introduces people to Christ and must be biblical; but the approach has to be different so they don't say "S.O.S." (Same Old Stuff). The Bible is so relevant, and we can take that relevancy in God's eternal Word and let the Holy Spirit work with it. Then preaching will be blessed by God, people will come to Christ, and the family will be nurtured.

Interviewer: Tell me about your process of preparing to stand in the pulpit.

Young: I am usually around twelve months ahead in planning my preaching menu. I publish its titles and the Scriptures involved, and we use them in handouts we give to our membership. I just preached through the Book of Ecclesiastes after about eight or nine months in Sunday morning worship.

I work at titles a great deal. I think a title is so important. It has to be relevant and it has to be alive, but it also has to say what the subject really is. For example, I preached a series on parenting from Mother's Day to Father's Day—a natural series for seven weeks. On Father's Day, I preached the last sermon. I preached on the father of the boy who was born blind, and I talked about exceptional children—those who are handicapped. I went through the whole range of different kinds of handicaps that people have. I called them "Exceptional People in the Family." The response was overwhelming.

I realized then that when I had preached the Bible before, I had talked about, "Here's someone born blind, here's someone who's deaf, lame, or whatever," and I jumped to the miracle. But we have to talk about those who live without a miracle. I dealt with that fact—that exceptional people living without a miracle are no less a miracle. I talked about different categories of exceptional people. I had the people stand and we prayed for those families. We thanked God for those exceptional people. It was a high moment of worship—a little different, but a high moment of worship.

I try to go through a book of the Bible verse by verse, and then I'll drop back and do a series like the one on parenting. I'm looking at a series on marriage in the autumn. In the very near future, I'll probably preach through Daniel, verse by verse.

I try to prepare well in advance. I get a bibliography—I'm book poor. Someone taught me a long time ago that you should spend as much money on books as you do on automobiles. In the first thirty years of my marriage, I spent a lot on old automobiles—so I've spent a lot on books! I really try to work at what I do. I'm old-fashioned. I write out a manuscript for what I do; I don't memorize it. I write it so it's mine. When it comes time to publish a book, I can just take my manuscripts and let someone clean up the poor English and the repetitions and it's ready to go, because I really work at that craft.

I preach without notes. If somebody asks, "What happens when you forget?" I say, "You keep talking until you remember—anybody knows that."

Interviewer: How do you prepare for that moment in the pulpit after you've written the manuscript?

Young: I used to practice some, though I rarely do that anymore; sometimes I will go over something. I get my outline and

> *The key to the process is discernment, plus taking all that information and saying it in a simple way.*

then I work on the transitional phrases. I spend a long time on the introduction and I spend a good while on the conclusion, then I begin to fill in the gaps. I'm now on Compuserve (a computer service), which is a wonderful help. I can find so many periodicals, speeches, press conferences, and TV or radio programs which commented on any one particular area I'm dealing with. I'm wired into various libraries from which I can get bibliographical information or a thesis that was written. This has been a recent thing for me, and it's opened up just a whole new world of information. The key to the process is discernment, plus taking all that information and saying it in a simple way.

For example, in order to meet those busters and those boomers, I think preaching needs to be void of much of the old religious terminology. Instead of talking about salvation, I might use the word *salvaged.* When you salvage something, you restore it for the purpose for which it was made—that's what salvaging is. That's also what salvation is. The boomer understands that. We have geared the pulpit in our church to those who are not yet there. We feed and minister to our flock through Bible study and through other kinds of worship experiences, but primarily we have pitched the ministry of our church to the secular mind.

Therefore, Ecclesiastes is right over the plate. We've had more adults come to Christ—more people who've come from being agnostics and atheists—just because of the Book of Ecclesiastes. It asks the question that the rest of the Bible answers. If you're going to teach the Bible, begin with Ecclesiastes.

I worked all last summer just on titles before I began in September. Then I worked on my outlines. I had my bibliography. I got people who had really struggled with Ecclesiastes ahead of me, which has always been helpful. Then I sit down with the Scriptures. First of all, I try to do my own work: "What does this Scripture say to me? Are there any pregnant words there?" I find those pregnant words and do a little word study. Then I try to let the Scripture outline itself, if that's possible. God works in creative ways and different ways in preaching.

My process of preparation: I get my sermon, my title, a sense of God's direction, then I write out manuscripts of that sermon and I preach without notes. I can just have an open Bible, because I've crafted that through writing. I dictate it before I preach. My sermon's typed before I preach, it's typed after I preach, so I've got double manuscripts for anything that I've done. It helps us to edit for television as well. I'll spend twenty hours a week on every sermon.

I'll preach twice every Sunday morning to two different congregations. We have Sunday school at 8:30, 9:40, and 11:00. I've got back-to-back worship services in the middle, at 9:40 and 11:00. Then we have the Sunday evening service at 6:00. So I'll preach generally twice a week. I'd like to preach once a week, but our Sunday evening worship has been so strong that it's hard to just do it once.

Interviewer: You mentioned using different sermon styles. For example, when you preach Daniel you'll take a verse-by-verse approach. What styles do you tend to use most frequently?

Young: The exegetical study is what I really enjoy, but I think you have to use plenty of illustrations and stories and you have to use application.

There's one problem I think many pastors have; I certainly have to grapple with it. I come from a rural Mississippi background, basically from a small town, and therefore I tend to tell stories about a cow or a horse or a field—old-fashioned stories that really don't relate to this generation. So I've gotten into the computer-crunching mode. You have to work on your vocabulary and stay up-to-date. I know a lot of great preachers who have dated themselves by their application or lack of application. I try to take something that is contemporary—for example, in my Ecclesiastes series I did a thing on "What would Jesus say to me now?" What would Jesus say to Michael Jordan? What would Jesus say to whomever? People listen to that. We have to stay up on it.

Interviewer: What particular challenges do you think preaching is facing in the '90s?

Young: I think apologetic preaching has to be the mode if we're going to get serious about reaching the secular person. I can stand up and say I believe this is what the Bible says—I believe it's the inerrant, authoritative Word of God—but by the same token, there'll be thousands of people out there in my congregation who don't automatically share that view. For example, on any given Sunday, we'll have over a thousand people in one of our three worship services who are not Christians and not members of our church—that many will be there every Sunday. Now if these people are going to hear and are going to listen, a lot of them would say, "You know, I don't know if I believe in God or

> *Relevant preaching that is evangelistic is going to have to be apologetic.*

not. I don't know if the Bible is really true." The purpose of preaching is to nurture and train the family of God—those who are already Christians—but I think relevant preaching that is evangelistic is going to have to be apologetic. About 25 or 30 percent of the preaching I do in my pulpit is apologetic—for those who don't believe.

You approach that in an entirely different way. For example, I'd say, "Do you believe there is evil in the world?" Here's someone having trouble with God, for example. And they'd say, "Yeah, there's evil in the world."

I'd say, "Well, logically if there's evil in the world, there's also good. So you believe that there's evil and there's good?"

"Well, yes."

"So, you believe there's moral law in the world."

"Yeah, if there's good and evil, there's moral law."

"Well, do you believe there's a moral lawgiver? Here's an effect, it has to have a cause."

"Yeah, there's a moral lawgiver."

All of a sudden they've bumped head-on into God! Particularly on great days like Christmas and Easter, when you have so many people who just come with family and friends, I take an apologetic approach. This approach is going to be relevant and alive and reaching people in the twenty-first century.

We have a marketplace ministry. We have a lot of support groups in my church for those who are HIV-positive. We call them the "Positive Christians." Our support groups are for those who have AIDS, those who are cancer victims, those who've lost children, those who have terminal illnesses. We have twenty-five to thirty support groups in our church. You can come from any part of Houston and, when you walk in, there will be somebody who'll say, "I'm ready to listen to you; I'm ready to love you." We listen and help.

We've forgotten several things about the characteristics of Jesus. Get in an average church and ask, "Name all the characteristics of Jesus." They'll say he was lovely, he was kind. One thing they'll often forget is he was a friend of sinners. We've forgotten that—how to be a friend to sinners. If you minister to people where they hurt, you don't have to worry about a chance to introduce them to Christ; they're going to ask you about coming to know Christ. They'll want to go to church with you. But you can't befriend them in some superficial way and "hang a scalp" on your wall. So I think the church needs to be there to minister, to love, and to nurture, and when people come in they find what the world's looking for: *life!*

We've seen almost two thousand people a year, from all walks of life, make their way up the aisles of our church. Part of the genius of that is my church family, not me—I'm the teacher and pastor and we've got a wonderful team. Preaching is a part of that, but worship is where we begin. Look at all these ministries out there that are nonthreatening. I hope we are always there with a cup of cold water or an activity that will make a difference.

A young Jewish lawyer in the largest law firm in Houston came to our electric light parade with his four-year-old son. We had a float, and the guy on the float waved at him and the boy said, "Daddy, who's that?" He said, "I think that's Joseph." "Who's Joseph?" "I think he's the father of Jesus." "Who's Jesus, Daddy?"

The little boy kept urging, "Daddy, let's go back there where Joseph waved at me during that parade. Let's go back there." A parade, of all things! This young man and his wife have come to Christ and been saved in the last few months. It all started at Christmas when their little boy said, "Joseph waved at me," and began to ask questions.

Too many churches spend all their time, I'm afraid, looking at their own navels—high steeple, few people churches. In our church, our people minister to one another because we seek to call forth their spiritual gifts. I'm just exercising my gift to get out of the way and let God do what he wants to do.

Interviewer: If you had the chance to counsel young preachers, what kind of counsel would you offer?

Young: When I was in college and God called me, an older pastor said, "If you ever decide to be a great preacher, all you have to do is walk on your knees." That's the best counsel I ever got. The highest calling is to be a Christian; and to those whom God singles out for a Christian vocation, I'd say, "Walk on your knees." It's the hardest work you do. You pray in secret, but there's no secret when you pray. You spend time with him, and time with his Word.

My devotional time is sort of different. I was taught, "Keep your devotional life separate from your preaching life." I do the very opposite. I want my devotional life to be directly tied to my preaching life so that when I stand up to exegete, to proclaim the truth, it has already ministered to me.

Another thing I would advise a young preacher, besides daily quiet time, would be to spend time in genuine study. A lot of people with natural gifts can stand up and preach several good sermons, but you must read widely. It's very important that you study exhaustively. I don't believe you can name a set of commentaries I do not own. I'm not a scholar by any stretch of the imagination, but when I deal with a text—to the extent of my ability with the tools that I have gotten from seminary—I exhaust that text. When you do that it lives; it comes alive for me, it is preached to me.

Remember, we're in the people business. When God's Word is honored, taught, proclaimed, then the Holy Spirit gives life—and people go where there's life. I say that churches should be fun, churches should be exciting. I'm the least likely person on the planet to be in the ministry, because as a young person church just bored me. I went through the motions. When I realized that God was working in my life and I answered his call on the campus of the University of Alabama, I said, "Lord, doing business with you is really exciting. Don't ever let me get bored or let me get boring, or let it be routine." And I've worked hard for that.

A final word of counsel: Many great preachers have preached with notes and read them. Harry Emerson Fosdick was a great communicator; John MacArthur and Chuck Swindoll are basically manuscript preachers. I contend that if you would take those same individuals and break them away from their notes and manuscripts, they would be so, so much better.

Also, I think you preach with your whole body; I think you preach with your eyes. I tell people to get away from the pulpit, except as a place to put your Bible. You need to be totally free. All three of my boys are basketball players. "To shoot free throws," I tell them, "you begin with the bottom of your feet." Every good shooter shoots from the bottom of their feet. You also preach from the bottom of your feet; you don't preach flat-footed. I think you have to have your whole body in it, and you communicate with your body. It's got to be natural or it can't be effective.

Two of my sons are in the ministry; my younger son is probably on his way there—he's still in college. When they took classes in speech, I said, "Don't let them mess with your style, with who you are, with your pronunciation. Just be yourselves." They're very quiet speakers. I heard James Smart at Southern Seminary; when he spoke, he would raise his voice into this little high-pitched thing so you listened to him. When I was in seminary at Southeastern, I heard George Buttrick speak, and Buttrick would pull on his earlobe; he did a lot of crazy things. Be yourself; that's what I would say.

November/December 1994